Australia Travel Guide 2024-2025

Top Destinations and Must-See Attractions in Australia

Augustus Whitman

TABLE OF CONTENTS:

TABLE OF CONTENTS:..1
COPYRIGHT PAGE..5
© Augustus Whitman, 2024..5
All rights reserved. 5
PREFACE...6
Chapter 1..16
INTRODUCTION TO AUSTRALIA.................................16
   Why Australia: An Overview of the Land Down Under..18
   Travel Planning: When to Go and How to Get Around...20
   Key Travel Tips: Weather, Safety, and Local Customs..23
   Visa and Entry Requirements for 2024-2025..........27
Chapter 2..30
SYDNEY AND NEW SOUTH WALES.........................30
   Iconic Sydney: Opera House, Harbour Bridge, and Bondi Beach..32
   The Blue Mountains: Scenic Drives, Bushwalks, and Lookouts..35
   Coastal Treasures: Byron Bay, Jervis Bay, and Whale Watching...39
   Off the Beaten Path: Hunter Valley Wineries and Outback Adventures...42
Chapter 3..45
BEST RESTAURANTS IN AUSTRALIA.......................45

Fine Dining in Sydney: Quay, Bennelong, and Tetsuya's..................47

Melbourne's Food Scene: Attica, Vue de Monde, and Laneway Gems......................50

Farm-to-Table in Tasmania: The Agrarian Kitchen, Franklin, and Wild Cuisine......................53

Top Spots in Regional Australia: Brisbane, Adelaide, and Perth's Culinary Delights.................. 56

Chapter 4..................... 59
BEST HOTELS IN AUSTRALIA...................... 59

Luxury Stays: Top 5-Star Hotels in Sydney and Melbourne...............61

Boutique Hotels: Unique Accommodations in Hobart, Adelaide, and Perth...................... 65

Eco-Friendly and Remote Stays: The Best Lodges in the Outback and Rainforest...................... 69

Budget-Friendly Options: Hostels, Guesthouses, and Affordable Stays Across Australia.......................... 72

Chapter 5..................... 76
OUTBACK AUSTRALIA AND THE NORTHERN TERRITORY................ 76

Uluru and Kata Tjuta: Sacred Landscapes and Indigenous Culture....................78

Alice Springs and Kings Canyon: Desert Adventures and Stargazing......................81

Darwin and Kakadu National Park: Wildlife, Waterfalls, and Wetlands.......................... 85

The Ghan Expedition: Iconic Train Journey Across the Outback........................... 89

Chapter 6..................... 93
WESTERN AUSTRALIA'S WILD WEST..................... 93

Perth: Beaches, Markets, and City Life................ 95
Margaret River and Wine Country: Vineyards, Surf, and Gourmet Foods..98
The Kimberley Region: Gorges, Waterfalls, and Remote Wilderness... 102
Ningaloo Reef: Swimming with Whale Sharks and Coral Coast Adventures...106

Chapter 7... 111

EMERGENCY CONTACTS AND SAFETY INFORMATION...111

Emergency Numbers: Police, Ambulance, and Fire Services.. 113
Embassy and Consulate Contacts for International Travelers... 115
Health Services: Hospitals, Clinics, and Pharmacies. 117
Travel Insurance and What to Do in Case of Emergency..119

Chapter 8... 124

BEST TIME TO VISIT AUSTRALIA..........................124

Australia's Seasons: A Breakdown of Climate and Regions..126
When to Visit for Wildlife: Whale Watching, Turtle Nesting, and More.. 129
Events and Festivals: Timing Your Trip for Australia's Best Celebrations... 132
Choosing the Perfect Time Based on Your Travel Style and Interests... 136

Chapter 9... 140

AUSTRALIA'S UNIQUE WILDLIFE AND NATURE.. 140

Meet the Marsupials: Kangaroos, Koalas, and

Tasmanian Devils..142

Birdwatching in Australia: From Parrots to Penguins. 145

Aquatic Wonders: Dolphins, Dugongs, and Marine Life...148

Conservation Efforts: Protecting Australia's Endangered Species.. 151

Chapter 10..156
DOS AND DON'TS IN AUSTRALIA.......................... 156

Dos for an Enjoyable Australian Trip: Cultural Etiquette and Safety Tips..158

Don'ts: Common Tourist Mistakes and How to Avoid Them...163

Respecting Indigenous Culture and Nature: What Every Visitor Should Know................................... 167

Practical Tips for Sustainable and Responsible Travel in Australia.............. 171

COPYRIGHT PAGE

© Augustus Whitman, 2024.

All rights reserved.

No part of this publication may be reproduced, stored or transmitted in any form or by any means, electronic, mechanical, photocopying, recording, scanning, or otherwise without written permission from the publisher. It is illegal to copy this book, post it to a website, or distribute it by any other means without permission

PREFACE

As I stood on the red soil of the Outback, the vastness of the Australian wilderness stretched before me like a canvas waiting to be painted with stories. This wasn't my first journey into the unknown, but it was the one I knew would change me forever. I had always been an explorer at heart, drawn to the edges of maps, to the places where few have ventured, but something about Australia called to me differently. It was more than the allure of its iconic landmarks, more than the promise of its famous wildlife. It was the land itself, raw and untamed, that seemed to invite me on a journey deeper than any I had undertaken before.

Australia is a place of extremes. From the dense, ancient rainforests of Queensland to the sun-bleached deserts of Western Australia, from the cosmopolitan bustle of Sydney to the quiet isolation of the Kimberley region, the country holds a diversity that few places on Earth can match. But this trip was not meant to be a checklist of destinations. I wasn't here to simply see the Great Barrier Reef or climb the Sydney Harbour Bridge, though I would do both. I came to Australia to understand it, to feel it in my bones, to let its stories seep into me as I traveled its dusty roads and sparkling coastlines.

It started, as all great adventures do, with an idea. What if I traveled all the way around Australia? Not just through the popular cities or along the tourist trails, but circumnavigate the continent, pushing myself to explore the most remote corners, to meet people whose lives were shaped by this land in ways I could hardly imagine. The more I thought about it, the more the idea consumed me. I started planning, mapping out a rough route that would take me through every state and territory, across deserts and through forests, from the wilds of Tasmania to the rugged cliffs of Cape York.

The first leg of my journey took me to the Northern Territory, to a place that felt as far from my world as possible. I stood before Uluru at sunrise, the massive sandstone monolith glowing in shades of red and orange that seemed impossible to describe. I had seen pictures of Uluru before, of course, but nothing prepared me for the sheer presence of it. The air around it felt thick with history, as if the rock itself was breathing the stories of the Anangu people who have lived there for thousands of years. I spent days exploring the area, hiking around the base of the rock, learning from the local Indigenous guides who shared their knowledge of the land, the flora and fauna, and the Dreamtime stories that give Uluru its spiritual significance.

As I moved south towards the Flinders Ranges in South Australia, the landscape began to change. The red earth gave way to rugged mountains and sweeping valleys. I had heard that the Flinders were some of the oldest mountains in the world, and walking through them felt like stepping back in time. There's something humbling about standing in a place that's existed for over 600 million years, a place that has witnessed the rise and fall of species, the shifting of continents. I camped under the stars, the night sky so clear that it felt like I could reach up and touch the Milky Way. The isolation was profound, but it wasn't lonely. The land had a way of keeping me company, whispering its stories in the wind, in the rustling of the eucalyptus leaves, in the call of a distant dingo.

One of the most surprising parts of my journey was the people I met along the way. Australians are a hardy, welcoming bunch, especially in the outback, where communities are often small and far apart. In the remote town of Coober Pedy, where most of the population lives underground to escape the relentless heat, I was invited into homes dug into the earth, where the temperature was always cool, no matter how scorching it was outside. Coober Pedy is known for its opals, and I spent a few days learning about the mining industry, even trying my hand at 'noodling' – searching for leftover gems in the piles of dirt discarded by the miners. I didn't find any opals worth keeping, but I did leave with a deep respect for the people who call this harsh environment home.

My journey continued west, through the Nullarbor Plain, an expanse so flat and desolate that it felt like I was driving across the surface of another planet. The road stretched out endlessly before me, with no sign of civilization for hours at a time. The emptiness was both exhilarating and terrifying. There were moments when I questioned why I had decided to undertake such a daunting journey, but then something remarkable would happen – a mob of kangaroos bounding across the road at dusk, or a wedge-tailed eagle soaring overhead – and I would remember why I was here. Australia, in its vastness, has a way of reminding you how small you are, and how beautiful that can be.

Western Australia, with its stunning coastline and remote interior, was a highlight of the trip. I swam with whale sharks off the Ningaloo Reef, an experience that left me breathless in more ways than one. These gentle giants, despite their size, moved through the water with such grace that I felt like an intruder in their world. On land, I explored the Pinnacles Desert, where strange limestone formations rise out of the sand like ancient sentinels, and hiked through Karijini National Park, where deep red gorges and cascading waterfalls seemed to appear out of nowhere in the middle of the arid landscape.

As I made my way down the west coast, through the lush wine regions of Margaret River and into the city of Perth, I began to realize that this journey was more than just an adventure. It was becoming a deeply personal exploration of not only Australia, but of myself. There is something about the isolation of the Outback, the vastness of the desert, the endless sky, that strips away all pretense. You are forced to confront yourself, to sit with your thoughts in a way that is uncomfortable but ultimately transformative. I had come to Australia to explore its landscapes, but in doing so, I was also uncovering parts of myself that I had long buried.

Crossing the southern coast, I ventured into the wilds of Tasmania. The island state, with its dense forests and rugged coastlines, felt like a world unto itself. I hiked through the Tarkine, one of the largest temperate rainforests in the world, where ancient trees towered above me and the air was thick with the scent of moss and earth. I camped along the Overland Track, a famous multi-day hike that took me through some of the most breathtaking scenery I had ever encountered – glacial lakes, alpine meadows, and craggy mountain peaks. Tasmania's beauty was almost overwhelming, and I found myself lingering there longer than I had planned, reluctant to leave the serenity of its wilderness.

But leave I did, heading north again, through Victoria and New South Wales, where I surfed the iconic beaches of the Great Ocean Road, explored the rainforests of the Blue Mountains, and finally made my way to Sydney. Standing on the steps of the Sydney Opera House, looking out over the sparkling waters of the harbour, I felt a sense of accomplishment. I had done it. I had traveled around Australia, from its most famous cities to its most remote outposts. But more than that, I had come to know a country that is as complex as it is beautiful, a place that is defined not only by its landscapes but by the people who live there, by the stories they carry with them, and by the deep, ancient history that pulses beneath the surface.

And that is why I wrote this book. Not just to document the places I visited or the adventures I had, but to share the stories of Australia – both the ones that have been told for thousands of years, and the ones that are being written every day. This country has a way of getting under your skin, of making you see the world in a new light. It challenges you, humbles you, and ultimately, it changes you.

In writing this book, I hope to bring some of that experience to my readers. I want them to feel the heat of the Outback, to smell the eucalyptus on the wind, to hear the laughter of the kookaburras at dawn. I want them to understand the deep connection that the Indigenous peoples of Australia have with the land, a connection that is as old as time itself. And most of all, I want them to see Australia not just as a destination, but as a living, breathing entity, full of stories waiting to be told. Because in the end, that's what exploration is all about –

not just seeing new places, but discovering the stories that make those places come alive.

Chapter 1

INTRODUCTION TO AUSTRALIA

Australia, often referred to as the "Land Down Under," is a country that captivates the hearts of travelers from all over the globe. Renowned for its stunning natural landscapes, Australia is home to diverse ecosystems ranging from the iconic Outback to lush rainforests and pristine beaches. The Great Barrier Reef, a UNESCO World Heritage Site, showcases an underwater paradise filled with vibrant coral reefs and marine life, attracting divers and snorkelers from around the world. Beyond its natural beauty, Australia's cities pulse with life and culture. Sydney dazzles with its architectural marvels, including the Sydney Opera House and Harbour Bridge, while Melbourne stands out for its artistic flair, café culture, and vibrant street art scene. Each city offers unique culinary experiences, whether it's indulging in fresh seafood by the coast or exploring multicultural food markets that reflect the country's diverse population.

In addition to its breathtaking landscapes and urban excitement, Australia boasts a rich cultural heritage that dates back over 65,000 years with the traditions of Aboriginal and Torres Strait Islander peoples. This deep-rooted history enriches the Australian experience, as travelers can engage in cultural tours, art exhibitions, and festivals that celebrate indigenous customs and stories. From exploring ancient rock art sites to participating in traditional ceremonies, visitors gain a profound appreciation for the country's past. As you plan your journey, it's essential to consider factors such as the best times to visit, how to navigate the vast regions, and local customs that will enhance your stay. This chapter aims to equip you with all the necessary information to ensure a smooth travel experience, including updated visa and entry requirements for 2024-2025, making your adventure in Australia both enjoyable and memorable.

Why Australia: An Overview of the Land Down Under

Australia is the world's sixth-largest country and is renowned for its breathtaking natural beauty, which ranges from pristine beaches and tropical rainforests to rugged outback and awe-inspiring mountains. It is also home to unique wildlife, including kangaroos, koalas, and the iconic platypus. The Great Barrier Reef, a UNESCO World Heritage Site, is the largest coral reef system in the world and offers incredible opportunities for snorkeling and scuba diving.

In addition to its natural wonders, Australia boasts vibrant cities rich in culture and history. Sydney, with its iconic Sydney Opera House and Harbour Bridge, is a bustling metropolis that serves as a gateway to Australia's diverse attractions. Melbourne, known for its arts scene, coffee culture, and multicultural population, consistently ranks as one of the world's most livable cities. Other significant urban centers like Brisbane,

Perth, and Adelaide each offer their own unique flavors and experiences.

Australia's indigenous heritage is another compelling aspect of the country. The Aboriginal and Torres Strait Islander peoples have lived on the continent for over 65,000 years, contributing to a rich tapestry of stories, art, and traditions. Visitors have the opportunity to learn about this ancient culture through various tours, galleries, and cultural events, providing a deeper understanding of Australia's identity.

Travel Planning: When to Go and How to Get Around

When to Go

Australia's vast size means that the climate varies significantly across regions, making it crucial for travelers to choose their timing based on their desired activities and destinations. Generally, the best time to visit is during the Australian spring (September to

November) and autumn (March to May), when the weather is pleasant and ideal for outdoor activities.

- Spring (September to November): This season brings blooming wildflowers, particularly in Western Australia. Temperatures are moderate, making it perfect for visiting cities and national parks.

- Summer (December to February): Known for its hot weather, summer is ideal for beachgoers but can be sweltering in the interior. Coastal cities like Sydney and Melbourne are lively with festivals and outdoor events.

- Autumn (March to May): Autumn provides comfortable temperatures and fewer tourists. It's an excellent time for wine tours in regions like the Barossa Valley and Margaret River.

- Winter (June to August): While winter can be chilly in the south, northern regions like Cairns and Darwin remain warm and attract visitors for their tropical climate and activities.

How to Get Around

Getting around Australia can be an adventure in itself. The country is well-connected by various transportation options, catering to both urban and rural travel.

- Domestic Flights: Given Australia's size, flying is often the quickest way to traverse long distances. Major airlines such as Qantas, Virgin Australia, and Jetstar offer extensive domestic routes. Booking in advance can secure lower fares.

- Driving: Renting a car or campervan is a popular choice for those who wish to explore at their own pace. Australia has a well-maintained network of highways and scenic routes, such as the Great Ocean Road and Pacific Coast Highway. However, be aware of wildlife crossing roads, especially at dusk and dawn.

- Public Transport: Major cities offer reliable public transport systems, including buses, trains, and trams.

Sydney and Melbourne, for instance, have comprehensive networks that are easy to navigate. For longer distances, coaches like Greyhound provide intercity travel options.

- Bicycles and Walking: Many cities are bike-friendly and offer dedicated cycling paths. Walking tours are also popular, especially in historic districts and national parks.

Key Travel Tips: Weather, Safety, and Local Customs

Weather

Australia experiences a diverse range of climates due to its size and geographical variations. Travelers should pack accordingly:

- Sun Protection: The Australian sun can be intense, even in cooler months. Sunscreen, sunglasses, and hats are essential for outdoor activities.

- Layered Clothing: Given the variations in climate, especially between regions, layered clothing is advisable. Coastal areas may be warm, while the interior can be cool, particularly at night.

- Insect Repellent: In tropical regions, especially during summer, mosquitoes can be prevalent. Packing insect repellent is advisable for outdoor excursions.

Safety

Australia is generally a safe destination for travelers. However, it's important to be aware of certain safety tips:

- Emergency Services: In case of emergencies, dial 000 for police, fire, or ambulance services. Each state and territory has its own police force, and local authorities are usually very responsive.

- Wildlife Precautions: While Australia's wildlife is fascinating, some animals can be dangerous. Follow signage in national parks, especially regarding snakes, spiders, and crocodiles. Always keep a safe distance from wildlife and adhere to park guidelines.

- Swimming Safety: Australia's beaches are beautiful, but be cautious of riptides and currents. Swim between the flags on patrolled beaches, and be mindful of marine life, such as jellyfish, in certain areas.

Local Customs

Understanding Australian customs and etiquette can enhance the travel experience:

- Tipping: Tipping is not mandatory in Australia, but rounding up the bill or leaving a small tip for exceptional service is appreciated.

- Slang and Language: Australians are known for their informal language and slang. Familiarizing yourself with common terms (like "arvo" for afternoon or "brekkie" for breakfast) can be fun and help you connect with locals.

- Respect for Indigenous Culture: Australia's indigenous heritage is a vital part of the national identity. Showing respect for Aboriginal customs, land, and art is encouraged. Visitors should educate themselves about the significance of cultural sites and participate in indigenous-led experiences where possible.

Visa and Entry Requirements for 2024-2025

Travelers planning to visit Australia should be aware of the visa and entry requirements, which can vary based on nationality and the purpose of the visit.

Visa Requirements

As of 2024-2025, most travelers will require a visa to enter Australia, with several types available depending on the purpose of travel:

- Visitor Visa (subclass 600): This visa allows tourists to stay in Australia for up to 12 months. It is suitable for those visiting for leisure or to visit family and friends. Applicants can apply online or through Australian embassies and consulates.

- Electronic Travel Authority (ETA) (subclass 601): This visa is available for travelers from certain countries, allowing them to stay in Australia for short visits (up to 3 months). It can be easily obtained online.

- eVisitor (subclass 651): Similar to the ETA, this visa is for passport holders from the European Union and several other European countries, allowing stays of up to 3 months.

- Working Holiday Visa (subclass 417): For young people aged 18 to 30 from eligible countries, this visa allows travelers to work and travel in Australia for up to 12 months.

It is crucial for travelers to check the specific visa requirements based on their nationality and intended length of stay. Visitors should ensure that their passport is valid for at least six months beyond their intended departure date from Australia.

COVID-19 Considerations

As of 2024, travelers should remain informed about any COVID-19-related entry requirements. Australia has made significant strides in managing the pandemic, but regulations may change, so checking the latest updates from the Australian Department of Home Affairs or the local embassy is advisable.

Travelers may need to provide proof of vaccination or undergo testing before entry, depending on the current health guidelines in place.

Chapter 2

SYDNEY AND NEW SOUTH WALES

Sydney, the glittering harbor city of Australia, is more than just a vibrant metropolis; it embodies the spirit of a region rich in both culture and natural beauty. As the capital of New South Wales (NSW), Sydney is a city that seamlessly blends modernity with heritage. Its skyline, dominated by the iconic Sydney Opera House and the Sydney Harbour Bridge, is a testament to architectural ingenuity and stands as a beacon for travelers worldwide. The Opera House, with its unique shell-like design, represents the artistic soul of the city, while the Harbour Bridge offers both a literal and symbolic connection between Sydney's buzzing urban center and its surrounding natural wonders. At the same time, Bondi Beach, with its golden sands and famous surf, reflects Sydney's laid-back, outdoor lifestyle. The beach culture here is not just about sunbathing and surfing but about enjoying the fusion of nature and city living, where vibrant cafes, art scenes, and bustling coastal markets create an atmosphere of relaxation and energy.

Beyond the urban allure, Sydney serves as the gateway to the breathtaking landscapes of New South Wales. Venture just an hour or two outside the city, and you'll find the rugged beauty of the Blue Mountains, where ancient rainforests, dramatic cliffs, and mist-covered valleys create a world ripe for exploration. This UNESCO World Heritage site offers an array of outdoor activities, from scenic drives to invigorating bushwalks. To the north, the Hunter Valley entices with its rolling vineyards and renowned wineries, where visitors can indulge in wine-tasting experiences amidst some of the country's finest Semillon and Shiraz. Along the coast, the pristine beaches of Jervis Bay and the bohemian charm of Byron Bay offer serene escapes, while marine life enthusiasts can enjoy some of the best whale-watching spots in the world. Whether you're captivated by Sydney's urban vibrancy or drawn to the natural splendor of its surroundings, this chapter is your guide to uncovering the diverse experiences that make Sydney and NSW an unforgettable destination.

Iconic Sydney: Opera House, Harbour Bridge, and Bondi Beach

Sydney Opera House

Few structures in the world are as immediately recognizable as the Sydney Opera House. Situated on Bennelong Point, its unique sail-like design was conceived by Danish architect Jørn Utzon and completed in 1973. Declared a UNESCO World Heritage site in 2007, the Opera House isn't just an architectural marvel but also a hub for the arts, hosting over 1,500 performances annually, ranging from opera and ballet to contemporary music and theater.

For visitors, a trip to the Opera House offers more than just a photo opportunity. Guided tours take you behind the scenes to explore its history, from the challenges of its construction to the cutting-edge technology used in performances today. For an elevated experience, book a show or dine at Bennelong, a fine-dining restaurant located within the Opera House, offering stunning views of the harbor.

Sydney Harbour Bridge

Spanning the glittering waters of Sydney Harbour, the Sydney Harbour Bridge is both an engineering masterpiece and a symbol of the city. Completed in 1932, it remains the world's largest steel arch bridge and is affectionately known as "The Coathanger" due to its distinctive shape. Walking across the bridge is a popular activity for visitors, offering panoramic views of the city skyline and harbor.

For thrill-seekers, the BridgeClimb is a must-do. Participants are strapped into safety gear and guided along the bridge's upper arch, reaching a height of 134 meters above sea level. The reward is one of the best views in the world—a sweeping panorama of Sydney's landmarks, the harbor, and the distant Blue Mountains.

Bondi Beach

No visit to Sydney is complete without a trip to Bondi Beach. This iconic stretch of golden sand is not only a haven for surfers but also a cultural hub known for its laid-back atmosphere. Located just 7 kilometers from the city center, Bondi Beach is perfect for sunbathing, swimming, and people-watching.

For those looking to get active, the Bondi to Coogee Coastal Walk is a 6-kilometer scenic trail that winds along the cliffs, offering stunning views of the Pacific Ocean. Along the way, you'll pass smaller beaches and coves, such as Tamarama and Bronte, each with its own charm.

Bondi also boasts a vibrant food scene. The streets surrounding the beach are lined with cafes, restaurants, and bars, many offering alfresco dining with ocean views. Whether you're grabbing a quick coffee or settling in for a seafood feast, Bondi's culinary offerings are as diverse as its beachside crowd.

The Blue Mountains: Scenic Drives, Bushwalks, and Lookouts

Just a 90-minute drive west of Sydney lies the Blue Mountains, a World Heritage-listed region known for its dramatic cliffs, lush rainforests, and cascading waterfalls. Named for the blue haze created by the vast eucalyptus forests, this area is a haven for nature lovers, offering a variety of outdoor activities, from scenic drives to challenging bushwalks.

Scenic Drives

The Great Western Highway and Bells Line of Road are two popular routes that wind through the Blue Mountains, offering spectacular views along the way. The Great Western Highway passes through towns like Leura and Katoomba, where you can stop to explore boutique shops, cafes, and art galleries. For a more off-the-beaten-path experience, take Bells Line of Road, which offers quieter roads and passes through the quaint town of Bilpin, famous for its apple orchards.

The drive to Govetts Leap Lookout is another must, providing one of the most breathtaking views in the region. The lookout offers sweeping vistas of the Grose Valley, where sheer cliffs plunge into dense forests, creating a dramatic and unforgettable landscape.

Bushwalks

The Blue Mountains are crisscrossed with over 140 kilometers of walking tracks, catering to all levels of fitness and experience. One of the most popular is the Three Sisters Walk, which takes you to an iconic rock formation that towers over the Jamison Valley. Legend has it that the three rock spires represent three sisters who were turned to stone by an Indigenous elder to protect them from harm.

For more seasoned hikers, the National Pass offers a challenging but rewarding trek. This 6-kilometer loop takes you along cliff edges, through dense forests, and past stunning waterfalls like Wentworth Falls. The combination of natural beauty and historic hand-carved stairways makes this walk a highlight of the Blue Mountains.

Lookouts

In addition to Govetts Leap, the Blue Mountains are home to numerous lookouts, each offering unique perspectives of the landscape. Echo Point, near Katoomba, is perhaps the most famous, providing close-up views of the Three Sisters and the vast Jamison Valley below. The lookout is also the starting point for several bushwalking trails.

Further afield, Sublime Point offers a quieter, less crowded alternative, with panoramic views of the valleys and cliffs that stretch as far as the eye can see. At sunset, the view from here is particularly magical as the light casts a warm glow over the rugged terrain.

Coastal Treasures: Byron Bay, Jervis Bay, and Whale Watching

The coastline of New South Wales is dotted with pristine beaches, charming towns, and abundant marine life. From the relaxed vibe of Byron Bay to the crystal-clear waters of Jervis Bay, the coastal treasures of this region are perfect for those seeking sun, surf, and sea life.

Byron Bay

Located on the far north coast of NSW, Byron Bay is a coastal town famous for its bohemian atmosphere, surf culture, and natural beauty. It's Australia's easternmost point, and a hike up to Cape Byron Lighthouse offers stunning views of the Pacific Ocean and the chance to spot dolphins and migrating whales.

Byron's Main Beach is perfect for swimming and surfing, while nearby Wategos Beach is a more secluded option, ideal for a peaceful day by the sea. The town itself is known for its eclectic mix of cafes, yoga studios, and art galleries, making it a hub for creative and free-spirited travelers.

For those looking to explore beyond the beach, the hinterland around Byron Bay is filled with lush rainforests, waterfalls, and charming towns like Bangalow, known for its artisan markets and historic architecture.

Jervis Bay

Jervis Bay, located about three hours south of Sydney, is renowned for having some of the whitest sand beaches in the world. The calm, turquoise waters of Hyams Beach are perfect for swimming, snorkeling, and paddleboarding. Jervis Bay is also a marine sanctuary, making it a prime spot for diving and encountering marine life such as dolphins, sea turtles, and rays.

One of the highlights of visiting Jervis Bay is the chance to go whale watching. Between May and November, humpback whales migrate along the coast, and Jervis Bay offers one of the best vantage points to witness this incredible natural event. Boat tours depart regularly, allowing visitors to get up close to these majestic creatures as they breach and play in the ocean.

Whale Watching

New South Wales is one of the best places in Australia to experience whale watching, with several prime locations along the coast. From Byron Bay in the north to Eden in the south, whales can be spotted during their annual migration along the east coast.

The best time to see whales is during the Australian winter months, from June to August, when humpback whales migrate north to breed in the warmer waters off Queensland. They return south between September and November, often with their calves in tow.

Many coastal towns, such as Coffs Harbour, Port Stephens, and Newcastle, offer whale-watching tours. These boat tours provide a close-up view of the whales as they breach, slap their tails, and sometimes even swim alongside the vessels.

Off the Beaten Path: Hunter Valley Wineries and Outback Adventures

While Sydney's cityscape and the NSW coastline draw most of the attention, there's a wealth of experiences waiting to be discovered off the beaten path. From the world-class vineyards of the Hunter Valley to the vast, rugged landscapes of the Outback, these destinations offer a deeper, more immersive exploration of New South Wales.

Hunter Valley Wineries

Just two hours north of Sydney, the Hunter Valley is Australia's oldest wine region, renowned for its production of premium Semillon, Shiraz, and Chardonnay. With more than 150 wineries in the area, wine enthusiasts can spend days exploring the vineyards, cellar doors, and gourmet restaurants that make this region a food and wine lover's paradise.

Many wineries offer tours and tastings, giving visitors the opportunity to learn about the winemaking process and sample some of the region's best vintages. Some of the top vineyards to visit include Tyrrell's, Brokenwood, and Audrey Wilkinson, each offering stunning views of the surrounding countryside.

In addition to wine tasting, the Hunter Valley is also known for its artisanal produce, including cheese, chocolate, and olive oil. A visit to the Hunter Valley Cheese Factory or a meal at one of the region's award-winning restaurants is the perfect complement to a day of wine tasting.

For a unique experience, consider taking a hot air balloon ride.

Chapter 3

BEST RESTAURANTS IN AUSTRALIA

Australia's culinary scene reflects the country's rich multicultural heritage and the diversity of its landscapes. Influenced by waves of immigration from Asia, Europe, and the Middle East, Australian cuisine blends these international flavors with native ingredients, creating a unique fusion that sets it apart on the global stage. From vibrant urban centers to remote regions, Australia's food culture is shaped by the availability of fresh, local produce, seafood from its expansive coastline, and indigenous ingredients that are now gaining recognition for their unique contributions to contemporary cuisine. The commitment to sustainability has also become central to the dining experience, with chefs increasingly emphasizing farm-to-table practices, foraging, and reducing food waste to ensure an environmentally conscious approach to cooking.

Whether indulging in fine dining at Sydney's world-class restaurants or enjoying the rustic charm of Tasmania's farm-to-table eateries, Australia offers a range of culinary experiences that cater to every palate. The country's top chefs are celebrated for their creativity and their ability to push the boundaries of traditional flavors, often combining unexpected ingredients and techniques to create innovative dishes. In regions like Melbourne, known for its dynamic food scene, and Perth, where coastal flavors take center stage, dining is more than just a meal—it's an exploration of place and culture. This chapter highlights some of the best dining experiences across Australia, from cutting-edge restaurants in its bustling cities to hidden gems in its scenic rural areas, showcasing the depth and breadth of the country's ever-evolving gastronomic landscape.

Fine Dining in Sydney: Quay, Bennelong, and Tetsuya's

Sydney is home to some of the finest restaurants in the world, with its glittering harbor serving as a backdrop to culinary excellence. This section delves into three of Sydney's most celebrated fine-dining establishments: **Quay**, **Bennelong**, and **Tetsuya's**, each offering unique experiences that define the city's high-end culinary scene.

Quay is often regarded as the crown jewel of Sydney's fine dining. Perched above Sydney Harbour, with sweeping views of the Sydney Opera House and the Harbour Bridge, Quay's location is rivaled only by its cuisine. Chef Peter Gilmore's innovative approach to Australian produce shines in dishes like the signature "Snow Egg" and "White Coral." Quay's menu changes seasonally, reflecting Gilmore's commitment to sourcing the freshest ingredients. Every dish is a work of art, combining intricate flavors and textures with breathtaking presentation. The restaurant's dedication to sustainability and creativity ensures it remains at the forefront of Australian gastronomy.

Equally iconic is **Bennelong**, located inside the Sydney Opera House. Headed by Chef Peter Gilmore as well,

Bennelong takes advantage of its extraordinary setting to offer a menu that celebrates the best of Australian cuisine. The architecture of the Opera House lends an air of grandeur to the dining experience, and the menu emphasizes native ingredients, often reinterpreting traditional Australian dishes with modern techniques. Bennelong's multi-course degustation menu is a culinary journey through Australia, with each dish reflecting the country's rich agricultural heritage. The dining experience here seamlessly integrates Australian culture, history, and modern fine dining.

Tetsuya's, located in the heart of Sydney, offers a blend of Japanese and French cuisine with an emphasis on meticulous preparation and exceptional flavors. Chef Tetsuya Wakuda has crafted a menu that focuses on the delicate balance of taste, texture, and visual appeal, with his signature confit of ocean trout being a staple of the restaurant's offerings. Tetsuya's utilizes a serene garden setting to create an atmosphere of calm, allowing diners to focus on the extraordinary food. The restaurant's degustation menu is a constantly evolving showcase of seasonal ingredients, prepared with precision and care. This fusion of Japanese simplicity with French techniques creates a truly unforgettable dining experience.

Melbourne's Food Scene: Attica, Vue de Monde, and Laneway Gems

Melbourne is widely considered the culinary capital of Australia, known for its vibrant food scene that spans fine dining, innovative cafes, and hidden laneway gems. The city's diverse population has fostered a fusion of international cuisines, making it a foodie paradise. In this section, we explore some of Melbourne's top restaurants, including the acclaimed **Attica**, **Vue de Monde**, and the city's hidden **laneway gems**.

Attica, led by Chef Ben Shewry, is consistently ranked among the best restaurants in the world. Located in the suburb of Ripponlea, Attica has become synonymous with creativity, sustainability, and indigenous Australian ingredients. Shewry's approach to cooking is deeply personal, often drawing inspiration from his upbringing in New Zealand and his passion for Australia's native flora and fauna. The tasting menu at Attica is an exploration of Australian produce, featuring ingredients such as bunya nuts, finger lime, and marron. The restaurant's commitment to sustainability extends to its kitchen garden, where many of the ingredients are grown on-site. Attica offers an immersive dining experience that is as thought-provoking as it is delicious, with each dish telling a story of the land and its people.

For those seeking a more luxurious dining experience, **Vue de Monde** offers unparalleled views of Melbourne's skyline and a menu that is a testament to the art of fine dining. Located on the 55th floor of the Rialto Tower, Vue de Monde combines modern Australian cuisine with French techniques, creating a dining experience that is both elegant and innovative. Chef Shannon Bennett is known for his attention to detail, and every aspect of the dining experience at Vue de Monde is meticulously crafted, from the seasonal degustation menu to the curated wine list. The restaurant's philosophy emphasizes the use of local and sustainable ingredients, and the dishes are often playful interpretations of classic flavors. With its breathtaking views and impeccable service, Vue de Monde is a must-visit for anyone seeking the pinnacle of Melbourne's fine dining.

While Melbourne is home to many high-end restaurants, some of the city's most exciting culinary experiences can be found in its **laneways**, where hidden gems offer a more casual, but no less memorable, dining experience. The city's laneways are packed with small eateries, each offering a unique take on global cuisine. From dumpling houses to modern Australian cafes, these hidden spots offer a more intimate glimpse into Melbourne's food culture. Some standout laneway spots include **Tonka**, a contemporary Indian restaurant tucked away in Duckboard Place, and **Bar Lourinhã**, a Mediterranean-inspired bar and eatery known for its vibrant atmosphere and share plates. Melbourne's laneways are where culinary experimentation meets casual dining, and they are a crucial part of the city's dynamic food scene.

Farm-to-Table in Tasmania: The Agrarian Kitchen, Franklin, and Wild Cuisine

Tasmania's pristine environment and rich agricultural heritage make it a haven for farm-to-table dining. The island's chefs take full advantage of the bounty of fresh produce, seafood, and artisanal products available to them, crafting menus that celebrate local ingredients. In this section, we highlight three of Tasmania's top dining destinations: **The Agrarian Kitchen**, **Franklin**, and the island's growing reputation for **wild cuisine**.

The Agrarian Kitchen in New Norfolk is a true farm-to-table restaurant, with much of its produce coming directly from the property's gardens and farm. Founded by Rodney Dunn and Séverine Demanet, the restaurant offers a rustic yet refined dining experience that focuses on seasonality and sustainability. The menu changes daily, depending on what is available from the garden, and dishes are crafted to highlight the natural flavors of the ingredients. The Agrarian Kitchen also offers cooking classes, allowing visitors to immerse themselves in the farm-to-table philosophy. The restaurant's dedication to organic and sustainable practices makes it a standout in Tasmania's burgeoning food scene.

Located in Hobart, **Franklin** is another must-visit for food lovers seeking a connection to the land. The restaurant's open kitchen and minimalist décor create a relaxed atmosphere, allowing the food to take center stage. Chef Analiese Gregory's approach to cooking is deeply influenced by her surroundings, with a focus on local ingredients, foraging, and preservation techniques. The menu at Franklin is ever-changing, depending on what is in season, and dishes often feature wild ingredients such as seaweed, wild garlic, and native herbs. Franklin is a celebration of Tasmania's natural beauty, with each dish reflecting the island's unique terroir.

Tasmania is also gaining a reputation for its **wild cuisine**, with chefs increasingly incorporating foraged ingredients into their menus. Wild ingredients such as mushrooms, herbs, and sea greens are used to create dishes that are both innovative and deeply rooted in the landscape. Restaurants like **Fico** in Hobart and **Templo** in Launceston have embraced this trend, offering menus that highlight the flavors of the wild. Foraging tours and wild food workshops are also becoming popular on the island, allowing visitors to experience the farm-to-table philosophy firsthand. Tasmania's wild cuisine is a testament to the island's deep connection to the land and its commitment to sustainability.

Top Spots in Regional Australia: Brisbane, Adelaide, and Perth's Culinary Delights

While Sydney and Melbourne often steal the spotlight, Australia's regional cities also boast thriving food scenes. In this section, we explore the top dining destinations in **Brisbane**, **Adelaide**, and **Perth**, where a new generation of chefs is making waves with innovative cuisine and a focus on local ingredients.

Brisbane's food scene has undergone a transformation in recent years, with an influx of new restaurants offering everything from casual eateries to fine dining. **Gerard's Bistro**, located in Fortitude Valley, is one of Brisbane's standout dining destinations. The menu, crafted by Chef Adam Wolfers, is inspired by Middle Eastern flavors, with a focus on share plates and bold spices. Dishes like the lamb shoulder with harissa and the smoked eggplant with tahini are perfect for sharing, and the restaurant's relaxed atmosphere makes it a favorite among locals. For those seeking a fine dining experience, **Esquire** offers a contemporary Australian menu with a focus on seasonal ingredients and innovative techniques.

In **Adelaide**, the food scene is dominated by local produce and a commitment to sustainability. **Orana**, led by Chef Jock Zonfrillo, is one of the city's top restaurants, offering a menu that celebrates indigenous Australian ingredients. Zonfrillo's commitment to working with native ingredients has earned Orana numerous accolades, and the restaurant's degustation menu is a journey through the flavors of Australia.

Dishes like kangaroo tail with wattleseed and native herbs showcase the diversity of the country's food culture, and the restaurant's intimate setting makes for a truly special dining experience. Adelaide is also home to a burgeoning wine scene, with nearby regions like the Barossa Valley producing some of the best wines in the country.

Perth has also emerged as a culinary hotspot, with a growing number of restaurants focusing on local seafood and produce. **Wildflower**, located atop the COMO The Treasury building, offers a fine dining experience that highlights the flavors of Western Australia. The menu is inspired by the six seasons of the indigenous Noongar calendar, with each dish reflecting the produce available during that time. Chef Matthew Sartori's focus on local ingredients and traditional cooking techniques makes Wildflower a standout in Perth's food scene. For a more casual experience, **Long Chim** offers authentic Thai street food in a vibrant setting, with dishes like pad Thai and green curry showcasing the bold flavors of Thailand.

Chapter 4

BEST HOTELS IN AUSTRALIA

Australia's accommodation landscape is a tapestry woven from diverse influences, reflecting the country's rich cultural heritage and breathtaking natural environments. In its major cities like Sydney and Melbourne, travelers can indulge in opulent 5-star hotels that offer not only luxurious amenities but also world-class dining and unparalleled service. These establishments often boast stunning views of iconic landmarks, allowing guests to immerse themselves in the vibrant urban culture while enjoying the utmost comfort. Beyond the cities, boutique retreats tucked away in picturesque locales offer a unique charm that combines local character with personalized service. These hotels often feature distinctive designs, incorporating regional art and architecture, and provide travelers with a more intimate experience that reflects the surrounding landscape.

For those seeking a deeper connection to nature, Australia is home to eco-lodges nestled in lush rainforests or rugged outback settings, where sustainable practices are at the forefront of the hospitality experience. These lodges allow guests to enjoy the breathtaking beauty of Australia's diverse ecosystems while minimizing their environmental impact. Moreover, budget-friendly guesthouses and hostels provide accessible options for travelers looking to explore the country without breaking the bank. These accommodations often foster a communal atmosphere, encouraging interaction among guests and offering valuable insights into local culture and attractions. In this chapter, we explore the best hotels across four main categories—luxury, boutique, eco-friendly, and budget—highlighting iconic establishments that stand out for their exceptional service, innovative design, and memorable guest experiences.

Luxury Stays: Top 5-Star Hotels in Sydney and Melbourne

For those looking to experience the pinnacle of luxury, both Sydney and Melbourne boast some of Australia's most impressive 5-star hotels. Known for their elegant design, high-end services, and prime locations, these hotels offer the best in comfort, style, and convenience, making them a favorite among discerning travelers.

In **Sydney**, the luxury hotel scene is epitomized by properties such as **Park Hyatt Sydney**, which offers an unrivaled location on the edge of Sydney Harbour, with stunning views of both the Opera House and Harbour Bridge. The hotel is known for its refined service, spacious rooms with floor-to-ceiling windows, and a rooftop pool that provides a serene oasis in the heart of the city. Park Hyatt's location makes it perfect for travelers wanting easy access to iconic landmarks, high-end shopping districts, and the city's finest dining options.

Another prominent name in Sydney's luxury accommodation scene is **The Langham Sydney**, which brings a mix of old-world elegance and modern comfort. With its sophisticated interiors, impeccable service, and renowned day spa, The Langham is ideal for guests seeking a retreat from the city's hustle and bustle. The hotel's central location in the historic Rocks district offers easy access to Sydney's vibrant arts and cultural scene, making it a popular choice for both international visitors and locals looking for a city escape.

Melbourne, renowned for its artistic flair and eclectic charm, is home to **Crown Towers Melbourne**, a symbol of opulence and grandeur. Located in the Southbank entertainment complex, Crown Towers offers luxury on a grand scale, with spacious rooms, world-class dining experiences, and an expansive casino. The hotel also features one of Melbourne's most sought-after spas, complete with a lavish pool area, ensuring that guests can relax and rejuvenate in style. With its proximity to the Yarra River and the city's bustling CBD, Crown Towers is perfect for both business and leisure travelers.

The Hotel Windsor in Melbourne stands as a testament to timeless elegance, offering guests a historic experience in a building that dates back to 1883. The Windsor's Victorian architecture, combined with modern amenities, creates a unique blend of past and present. Known for its traditional afternoon tea service and plush rooms, The Windsor provides a more classical alternative to Melbourne's modern hotel offerings. Located near Parliament House and the city's theater district, it is ideally positioned for those wanting to explore Melbourne's cultural highlights.

For travelers seeking sleek modernity, **Sofitel Melbourne on Collins** provides luxury with a contemporary twist. The hotel's high-rise location offers panoramic views of Melbourne's skyline, and its design-forward approach is reflected in its minimalist yet luxurious rooms. Sofitel's French-inspired gastronomy, excellent customer service, and prime location on Collins Street make it a standout in Melbourne's competitive luxury hotel market.

Boutique Hotels: Unique Accommodations in Hobart, Adelaide, and Perth

For travelers seeking something more intimate and personalized, Australia's boutique hotel scene offers unique accommodations that provide a distinct local flavor. Whether it's the charm of Tasmania's natural beauty or the vibrant energy of Western Australia's capital, boutique hotels in Hobart, Adelaide, and Perth provide an enriching experience for those wanting to stay somewhere with character.

In **Hobart**, **The Henry Jones Art Hotel** is a perfect example of how history and contemporary design can merge to create an unforgettable stay. This boutique hotel is housed in a former jam factory on Hobart's waterfront and has been converted into a stunning space that celebrates Tasmania's burgeoning art scene. With more than 400 pieces of contemporary art displayed throughout the hotel, each room feels like a gallery in itself. The Henry Jones also features exposed stone walls and timber beams, preserving the building's industrial heritage while providing all the modern comforts expected from a top boutique hotel.

Also in Hobart is the **MACq 01 Hotel**, a luxury storytelling hotel that highlights Tasmania's rich history through design and experience. Each room is themed around a character from Tasmania's past, from indigenous leaders to infamous convicts, blending the island's unique history with contemporary luxury. With its location on the waterfront and proximity to the Salamanca Markets, MACq 01 offers visitors an immersive Tasmanian experience while providing top-notch service and amenities.

Adelaide, South Australia's vibrant capital, offers an emerging boutique hotel scene with unique options like **The Mayfair Hotel**. Located in a restored heritage building, The Mayfair exudes old-world charm with a modern twist. The hotel is known for its luxurious rooms and stylish rooftop bar, Hennessy, which offers spectacular views of the Adelaide skyline. With its central location, The Mayfair is a short walk from Adelaide's shopping, arts precincts, and cultural landmarks, making it a favorite for those wanting to explore the city in style.

For something more intimate, **Mount Lofty House**, located in the Adelaide Hills, offers a boutique hotel experience amidst stunning natural surroundings. Known for its luxurious suites, spa facilities, and award-winning dining at Hardy's Verandah Restaurant, Mount Lofty House combines modern amenities with the tranquility of the Adelaide Hills, making it an excellent choice for travelers looking for a countryside retreat without sacrificing luxury.

In **Perth**, **COMO The Treasury** sets the standard for boutique luxury. Located in a restored 19th-century state treasury building, COMO The Treasury combines historic charm with modern luxury. The hotel features spacious rooms with high ceilings, elegant furnishings, and a renowned wellness spa. Its location in Perth's Cathedral Square places guests in the heart of the city, with easy access to boutique shopping, cultural attractions, and the city's burgeoning dining scene. The hotel's fine dining restaurant, Wildflower, is one of the best in the city, known for its seasonal menu inspired by the indigenous Noongar calendar.

For a more laid-back boutique experience, **Alex Hotel**, located in the vibrant Northbridge district of Perth, offers a contemporary and welcoming atmosphere. Known for its minimalist design and cozy communal spaces, Alex Hotel is a favorite among travelers who appreciate style without pretense. The rooftop terrace offers stunning views of the Perth skyline, while the hotel's proximity to cultural institutions like the Perth Cultural Centre and Art Gallery of Western Australia makes it an ideal base for exploring the city's artistic side.

Eco-Friendly and Remote Stays: The Best Lodges in the Outback and Rainforest

Australia's stunning landscapes and unique ecosystems have led to the rise of eco-friendly and remote lodges that offer luxury with a focus on sustainability. These lodges provide travelers with the opportunity to immerse themselves in Australia's natural beauty, from the vastness of the Outback to the lush rainforests of Queensland, all while ensuring minimal environmental impact.

One of the most iconic eco-lodges in Australia is **Longitude 131**, located near **Uluru** in the Northern Territory. This luxury wilderness camp offers an immersive experience in the heart of the Australian Outback, with views of the majestic Uluru and Kata Tjuta from each of the lodge's tented pavilions. Longitude 131 is renowned for its commitment to sustainability, incorporating solar energy, water conservation, and eco-friendly building materials into its design. Guests can enjoy exclusive tours of Uluru-Kata Tjuta National Park, where they'll learn about the area's indigenous culture and natural history, while dining under the stars in one of the most breathtaking settings in the world.

In **Queensland's Daintree Rainforest**, **Silky Oaks Lodge** offers a luxury eco-retreat surrounded by ancient rainforest and the pristine Mossman River. This lodge is designed to blend seamlessly with its environment, using sustainable materials and practices to minimize its footprint. Silky Oaks Lodge offers a range of nature-based activities, including guided rainforest walks, river snorkeling, and visits to the nearby Great Barrier Reef. The lodge's Treehouse Restaurant serves gourmet meals crafted from local and organic ingredients, offering guests a taste of the region's fresh produce. Silky Oaks Lodge is the perfect destination for travelers seeking both adventure and relaxation in one of Australia's most unique ecosystems.

For those looking to explore Australia's **Blue Mountains**, **Emirates One&Only Wolgan Valley** is a luxury eco-lodge that offers a remote, conservation-focused experience in the heart of New South Wales' bushland. Set on a 7,000-acre nature reserve, this lodge offers private villas with plunge pools, wildlife tours, and horse riding through the valley's rugged terrain. The lodge's commitment to sustainability is evident in its solar power system, use of locally sourced materials, and wildlife conservation efforts. Guests at Wolgan Valley can enjoy spa treatments, gourmet dining, and a range of outdoor activities, all while contributing to the preservation of Australia's unique flora and fauna.

Budget-Friendly Options: Hostels, Guesthouses, and Affordable Stays Across Australia

While Australia is home to many luxury and boutique hotels, it also offers a wide range of budget-friendly accommodations, from hostels to guesthouses and motels, catering to backpackers, students, and budget-conscious travelers. These affordable stays provide clean, comfortable lodging without sacrificing quality, allowing travelers to explore the country without breaking the bank.

In major cities like **Sydney**, **Wake Up! Sydney Central** is a popular choice among backpackers and budget travelers. Located near Central Station, this hostel offers modern facilities, clean dorms and private rooms, and a lively social atmosphere. With organized events, a rooftop bar, and a communal kitchen, Wake Up! Sydney is an ideal spot for travelers looking to meet new people and explore the city on a budget.

In **Melbourne**, **The Nunnery** in Fitzroy offers a charming and affordable stay in a former convent. This budget accommodation provides both dormitory and private rooms, a communal kitchen, and free breakfast. Its location in the hip Fitzroy neighborhood makes it a great base for exploring Melbourne's alternative arts scene, trendy cafes, and vintage shops.

For those exploring Australia's more remote regions, guesthouses and motels offer budget-friendly options. In **Tasmania**, **The Pickled Frog** in Hobart provides affordable accommodations with a laid-back atmosphere. Located in a historic building, this hostel offers dorms and private rooms, free shuttle services to nearby attractions, and a welcoming communal space where guests can relax after a day of exploring the island.

In **Cairns**, a gateway to the Great Barrier Reef, **Gilligan's Backpacker Hotel & Resort** is a well-known hostel that offers a mix of budget accommodation, a large outdoor pool, and a lively bar scene. This hostel caters to young travelers and backpackers looking for a social and affordable stay while exploring Queensland's tropical north.

For a more peaceful retreat, **Albany Backpackers** in **Western Australia** offers budget accommodation in a scenic location near the rugged coastline. With its friendly atmosphere, clean rooms, and proximity to attractions like **Torndirrup National Park**, Albany

Backpackers is perfect for travelers exploring Australia's natural beauty on a budget

Chapter 5

OUTBACK AUSTRALIA AND THE NORTHERN TERRITORY

The Northern Territory is often described as the beating heart of Australia, a place where ancient Indigenous traditions intertwine with the striking beauty of its natural landscapes. Home to some of the most recognizable landmarks in the country, such as Uluru and Kata Tjuta, this region offers travelers a profound connection to the land's cultural heritage. The Anangu people, traditional custodians of these sacred sites, share their rich stories and teachings, allowing visitors to engage with the spiritual significance of the area. Beyond the iconic monoliths, the Northern Territory is a treasure trove of diverse ecosystems, from arid deserts to lush wetlands, providing a haven for unique wildlife. This vibrant environment fosters a range of outdoor activities, including hiking, wildlife spotting, and stargazing, making it an ideal destination for adventure seekers and nature lovers alike.

This chapter explores four key areas that showcase the Northern Territory's remarkable offerings. Starting with Uluru and Kata Tjuta, readers will discover the cultural and spiritual importance of these landscapes, along with the various ways to experience their beauty. Next, Alice Springs and Kings Canyon present an intriguing mix of modern culture and ancient traditions, with opportunities for adventure in stunning natural settings. The tropical city of Darwin and the breathtaking Kakadu National Park highlight the region's rich biodiversity and Indigenous heritage, offering visitors a chance to explore lush wetlands and encounter wildlife in its natural habitat. Finally, the iconic Ghan Expedition provides a unique perspective on the Outback, connecting these diverse locations through an unforgettable train journey. Each section aims to provide an insightful and comprehensive guide for those eager to explore one of Australia's most enchanting and culturally rich regions.

Uluru and Kata Tjuta: Sacred Landscapes and Indigenous Culture

Uluru, also known as Ayers Rock, is perhaps Australia's most iconic natural landmark, a massive sandstone monolith rising dramatically from the surrounding plain. Situated in Uluru-Kata Tjuta National Park, this sacred site holds immense cultural significance for the Anangu people, the traditional custodians of the land. Uluru is not only a breathtaking geographical feature but also a central part of Anangu culture and spirituality, with countless stories interwoven with the landscape, known as Tjukurpa or the Dreamtime.

Visiting Uluru offers a unique opportunity to engage with Indigenous culture through guided tours led by Anangu guides who share their deep knowledge of the land. These experiences can range from cultural walks around the base of the rock to storytelling sessions that impart the rich history and significance of the site. One of the best ways to experience Uluru is during sunrise or sunset, when the rock changes colors in a spectacular display, illuminating the surrounding desert landscape. The **Field of Light**, an art installation by Bruce Munro, is another must-see, consisting of over 50,000 solar-powered lights that bloom like flowers in the desert, creating a stunning visual spectacle after dark.

Just a short drive from Uluru lies **Kata Tjuta**, also known as the Olgas, a group of large, domed rock formations that are just as significant to the Anangu people. The **Valley of the Winds Walk** provides breathtaking views of the domes and the opportunity to witness diverse flora and fauna in their natural habitats. The area is also rich in wildlife, and visitors might spot kangaroos, wallabies, and various bird species. The importance of these landscapes is emphasized by the park's commitment to conservation and the protection of the natural environment, making it an essential visit for those interested in Australia's unique ecology.

In addition to the natural beauty and cultural significance of Uluru and Kata Tjuta, the region offers various accommodation options that range from luxury lodges to campgrounds, providing visitors with diverse experiences. The **Sails in the Desert** hotel, for example, combines luxury with a deep appreciation for Indigenous culture, featuring artwork and decor that reflect the local heritage. For a more immersive experience, the **Longitude 131°** glamping site offers luxury tents with stunning views of Uluru and direct access to cultural experiences.

Travelers to Uluru and Kata Tjuta are encouraged to be respectful of the land and its cultural significance. Climbing Uluru is now prohibited to honor the wishes of the Anangu people, who regard the rock as sacred. Instead, visitors are invited to engage with the land through guided experiences that foster understanding and respect for Indigenous culture, providing an enriching journey into one of Australia's most revered landscapes.

Alice Springs and Kings Canyon: Desert Adventures and Stargazing

Nestled in the heart of the Outback, **Alice Springs** serves as a gateway to some of the Northern Territory's most extraordinary landscapes. Known for its rich history and vibrant art scene, this town has evolved from a telegraph station into a bustling community that offers a unique blend of modern amenities and traditional culture. The surrounding landscape is characterized by rugged terrain, stunning gorges, and expansive desert vistas, making it an ideal base for outdoor adventures.

One of the most popular activities in Alice Springs is exploring the nearby **MacDonnell Ranges**, a stunning stretch of mountains that offers numerous hiking and biking opportunities. The **Simpsons Gap**, **Standley Chasm**, and **Ormiston Gorge** are just a few of the breathtaking spots within the ranges, each featuring distinctive rock formations and native wildlife. Hiking trails vary in difficulty, catering to all fitness levels, and many offer opportunities to swim in waterholes and spot local fauna such as rock wallabies and various bird species.

Stargazing in Alice Springs is another unforgettable experience, thanks to the clear desert skies and minimal light pollution. The region is renowned for its breathtaking night skies, where visitors can witness constellations that are not easily visible in urban areas. Several local operators offer guided astronomy tours, providing telescopes and expert knowledge to enhance the experience. The **Alice Springs Telegraph Station Historical Reserve** is an excellent spot for an evening under the stars, combining history with the natural beauty of the surrounding landscape.

A short drive from Alice Springs, **Kings Canyon** offers one of the most stunning natural attractions in the Northern Territory. The **Kings Canyon Rim Walk** is a must-do for adventurous travelers, taking approximately three to four hours to complete. This hike provides panoramic views of the canyon's sandstone cliffs, lush gardens, and the chance to explore the Garden of Eden, a permanent waterhole surrounded by cycads and gum trees. The towering walls of Kings Canyon, which rise 100 meters above the canyon floor, create a dramatic backdrop for photography and reflection.

For those seeking a more leisurely experience, the **Kings Creek Walk** offers a shorter, easier option that allows visitors to enjoy the beauty of the canyon without the strenuous hike. After a day of exploring, accommodations range from campgrounds to luxury lodges, such as **Kings Canyon Resort**, which offers comfortable amenities and stunning views of the surrounding landscape. Whether you're hiking, stargazing, or immersing yourself in local culture, Alice Springs and Kings Canyon offer unforgettable experiences that showcase the best of the Outback.

Darwin and Kakadu National Park: Wildlife, Waterfalls, and Wetlands

As the capital of the Northern Territory, **Darwin** is a vibrant city that serves as the gateway to some of

Australia's most incredible natural wonders. With its tropical climate, stunning waterfront, and rich multicultural community, Darwin offers a unique blend of experiences for visitors. The city is known for its relaxed atmosphere, outdoor markets, and the opportunity to explore nearby national parks that showcase the region's stunning landscapes and wildlife.

Kakadu National Park, located just a few hours from Darwin, is a UNESCO World Heritage site that boasts an extraordinary diversity of ecosystems, including wetlands, rivers, and sandstone escarpments. The park is home to a rich array of wildlife, including saltwater crocodiles, kangaroos, and a variety of bird species, making it a paradise for nature enthusiasts and wildlife photographers. The best time to visit Kakadu is during the dry season, from May to October, when the weather is more favorable for exploration.

Visitors to Kakadu can embark on guided tours that offer insights into the park's rich Indigenous culture and natural history. One of the park's highlights is **Ubirr**, where ancient rock art can be found in stunning cliff-top galleries. The art depicts the cultural stories of the Indigenous people who have inhabited the area for thousands of years and offers a glimpse into their connection with the land. The **Nourlangie Rock** art site is another important location, featuring paintings that are over 20,000 years old, highlighting the enduring legacy of Indigenous culture in the region.

Kakadu is also known for its spectacular waterfalls, which cascade dramatically during the wet season and offer refreshing swimming opportunities in natural pools. The **Jim Jim Falls** and **Twin Falls** are among the most famous, accessible via 4WD tracks that wind through the rugged terrain. The waterfalls provide not only breathtaking views but also a chance to relax and enjoy the tranquility of nature.

In addition to Kakadu, **Litchfield National Park** is another popular destination for those looking to explore the natural beauty of the Northern Territory. Known for its cascading waterfalls, natural swimming holes, and lush rainforest, Litchfield offers a range of activities, including bushwalking, swimming, and wildlife spotting. The **Florence Falls** and **Wangi Falls** are particularly popular, providing stunning scenery and opportunities for a refreshing dip in crystal-clear waters.

Back in Darwin, the city offers a variety of accommodations, from luxury hotels to budget-friendly options, making it a great base for exploring the surrounding natural attractions. The Darwin Waterfront Precinct features restaurants, shops, and a lagoon, providing a lively atmosphere for dining and relaxation. The **Museum and Art Gallery of the Northern Territory** showcases the region's history, art, and natural heritage, while the **Mindil Beach Sunset Market** offers a vibrant experience with food stalls, local crafts, and live entertainment.

As a vibrant and diverse city, Darwin serves as an excellent launching point for exploring the natural wonders of the Northern Territory. With its unique blend of urban culture and stunning natural landscapes, the region offers a wealth of experiences for every type of traveler.

The Ghan Expedition: Iconic Train Journey Across the Outback

The Ghan Expedition is one of the most iconic train journeys in the world, traversing the heart of Australia from **Darwin** to **Adelaide** over a distance of nearly 3,000 kilometers. Named after the Afghan camel drivers who played a significant role in opening up the Australian interior during the 19th century, The Ghan offers travelers a unique perspective of the Outback, showcasing its breathtaking landscapes, rich history, and diverse cultures.

The journey begins in Darwin, where passengers board the luxurious train for an unforgettable adventure through the Northern Territory and South Australia. The Ghan features a range of accommodation options, from comfortable recliner seats in the economy class to luxurious gold and platinum service cabins that offer spacious sleeping quarters and private en-suite bathrooms. Each class provides a unique experience, with gourmet dining options and stunning views of the changing landscape.

As the train winds its way through the Outback, passengers are treated to breathtaking vistas of red deserts, rocky ranges, and sprawling cattle stations. The journey includes stops at iconic locations such as **Alice Springs** and **Katherine**, allowing travelers to explore the unique attractions of these towns. In Alice Springs, passengers can visit the **Alice Springs Desert Park** to learn about the desert environment and Indigenous culture, or take a scenic flight over the stunning MacDonnell Ranges. In Katherine, the stunning **Katherine Gorge** offers opportunities for boat cruises, canoeing, and guided walks, allowing passengers to immerse themselves in the natural beauty of the region.

One of the highlights of The Ghan experience is the chance to engage with local culture and history. The train often hosts guest speakers and cultural performances, providing insights into the Indigenous heritage of the land and the stories of the early pioneers who settled the Outback. Passengers can also participate in guided tours and excursions during the stops, enhancing their understanding of the diverse landscapes and communities they encounter along the way.

As the train continues south, it traverses the arid desert landscapes of the Outback, passing through vast cattle stations and ancient rock formations. The journey culminates in **Adelaide**, where passengers disembark to explore the charming capital of South Australia. Known for its vibrant arts scene, stunning parks, and renowned wine regions, Adelaide offers a fitting end to the remarkable journey.

Traveling aboard The Ghan is more than just a train ride; it is an immersive experience that allows travelers to connect with the spirit of the Outback and gain a deeper appreciation for Australia's diverse landscapes and cultures. With its luxurious accommodations, exceptional service, and breathtaking scenery, The Ghan

Expedition stands as a testament to the enduring allure of the Australian Outback.

Chapter 6

WESTERN AUSTRALIA'S WILD WEST

Western Australia (WA) is a vast and stunningly diverse region that captivates visitors with its breathtaking landscapes, vibrant cities, and rich Indigenous culture. Stretching over 2.6 million square kilometers, WA is home to some of Australia's most iconic destinations, including the bustling capital city of Perth. Here, visitors can experience a cosmopolitan atmosphere filled with trendy cafes, vibrant nightlife, and beautiful beaches like Cottesloe and Scarborough. Just a short drive from the city lies the renowned Margaret River wine region, famous for its exceptional wineries, artisanal food producers, and stunning coastal scenery. The Margaret River region offers an enticing blend of gourmet dining, outdoor adventures, and pristine beaches, making it a haven for food and wine enthusiasts alike.

Further afield, the rugged beauty of the Kimberley region reveals a land of dramatic gorges, ancient rock art, and cascading waterfalls. This remote wilderness is a treasure trove of natural wonders, from the majestic Bungle Bungles in Purnululu National Park to the stunning Horizontal Falls. The Kimberley is not only a place for outdoor adventures but also a cultural experience, with Indigenous communities offering insights into their rich history and connection to the land. Meanwhile, the pristine marine environment of Ningaloo Reef beckons snorkelers and divers to explore its vibrant coral gardens and swim alongside majestic whale sharks. This chapter will delve into these four key areas, highlighting the unique attractions, activities, and experiences that make Western Australia an unforgettable destination for travelers seeking adventure, culture, and natural beauty.

Perth: Beaches, Markets, and City Life

Perth, the capital of Western Australia, is a vibrant city known for its stunning beaches, lively arts scene, and relaxed lifestyle. Nestled between the Indian Ocean and the picturesque Swan River, Perth boasts a Mediterranean climate, making it an ideal destination year-round. The city offers a unique blend of modern urban life and natural beauty, with a range of attractions that cater to various interests.

One of the main draws of Perth is its beautiful beaches. **Cottesloe Beach**, with its soft sands and clear waters, is a favorite among locals and visitors alike. This iconic beach is perfect for swimming, sunbathing, or enjoying a meal at one of the nearby cafes. The sunset views over the Indian Ocean are particularly spectacular, making it a popular spot for evening gatherings. For those seeking a more tranquil experience, **Scarborough Beach** offers a more relaxed atmosphere, with ample opportunities for surfing, beach volleyball, and beachside dining.

Perth's cultural landscape is equally impressive, with a variety of galleries, museums, and performing arts venues. The **Art Gallery of Western Australia** showcases an extensive collection of Australian and

Indigenous art, while the **Western Australian Museum Boola Bardip** provides fascinating insights into the state's natural and cultural history. The **Perth Cultural Centre**, located in Northbridge, is a hub for arts and entertainment, hosting various festivals, live performances, and exhibitions throughout the year.

For those looking to immerse themselves in local culture, Perth is home to a range of markets that highlight the region's produce and artisanal goods. The **Fremantle Markets**, housed in a historic building, feature a diverse array of stalls selling fresh produce, handmade crafts, and unique souvenirs. Visitors can sample local delicacies, enjoy live music, and soak up the vibrant atmosphere of this bustling market. The **Perth City Farm** is another must-visit, offering fresh organic produce and community events that celebrate sustainable living.

Beyond its urban offerings, Perth serves as a gateway to numerous outdoor adventures. The nearby **Swan Valley** is Western Australia's oldest wine region, famous for its wineries, breweries, and gourmet food producers. Visitors can embark on wine tours, sample local cheeses, and enjoy farm-to-table dining experiences while taking in the picturesque countryside. The **Crawley Edge Boatshed**, known as the "Blue Boat House," is another popular spot, offering a scenic backdrop for photography and leisurely walks along the river.

As night falls, Perth comes alive with a vibrant nightlife scene. The **Northbridge** district is known for its array of bars, clubs, and restaurants, providing an eclectic mix of dining and entertainment options. From rooftop bars with stunning city views to live music venues showcasing local talent, Perth's nightlife has something for everyone. Whether relaxing on the beach, exploring cultural sites, or enjoying the lively atmosphere of the city, Perth offers a dynamic blend of experiences that capture the essence of Western Australia.

Margaret River and Wine Country: Vineyards, Surf, and Gourmet Foods

Margaret River, located about three hours south of Perth, is a premier destination renowned for its world-class wineries, stunning coastline, and vibrant food scene. This picturesque region has become synonymous with high-quality wine production, boasting over 200 vineyards that produce award-winning reds, whites, and sparkling wines. The area's unique geography, with its Mediterranean climate and fertile soil, creates ideal conditions for viticulture, attracting wine enthusiasts from around the globe.

A visit to Margaret River would be incomplete without indulging in a wine tour. Numerous companies offer guided tours that allow visitors to explore the region's finest wineries, many of which feature cellar doors where tastings are held. Some of the most celebrated wineries include **Vasse Felix, Leeuwin Estate**, and **Cullen Wines**, each offering unique tasting experiences paired with local cheeses and charcuterie. Many of the wineries also host gourmet restaurants, allowing visitors to savor exceptional food while enjoying stunning views of the vineyards.

In addition to its thriving wine scene, Margaret River is also known for its breathtaking coastal landscapes. The **Margaret River Surf Reef** attracts surfers from around the world, offering consistent waves and pristine beaches. **Prevelly Beach** is a popular spot for both surfers and beachgoers, with its picturesque setting and opportunities for swimming, fishing, and picnicking. The **Cape Naturaliste and Cape Leeuwin Lighthouses** provide excellent vantage points for coastal views, and the surrounding national parks offer a range of hiking trails that showcase the region's diverse flora and fauna.

The food scene in Margaret River is equally impressive, with a strong emphasis on local produce and sustainability. The region is home to artisanal cheese makers, chocolatiers, and gourmet food producers, making it a haven for food lovers. The **Margaret River Farmers Market,** held every Saturday, showcases fresh seasonal produce, homemade goods, and local specialties, providing visitors with an authentic taste of the region. Culinary workshops and cooking classes are also popular, offering opportunities to learn from local chefs and create delicious dishes using fresh ingredients.

For those looking to explore the natural beauty of Margaret River, the **Leeuwin-Naturaliste National Park** features stunning coastal cliffs, tranquil forests, and scenic walking trails. The **Cape to Cape Track**, a 135-kilometer trail that stretches from Cape Naturaliste to Cape Leeuwin, offers breathtaking views of the coastline and access to secluded beaches and hidden coves. The region's diverse landscapes make it an ideal destination for outdoor activities, including hiking, cycling, and whale watching during the migration season.

As a destination that seamlessly blends wine, food, surf, and nature, Margaret River offers visitors a chance to experience the best of Western Australia's culinary and outdoor offerings. Whether indulging in a wine tasting, savoring fresh local produce, or enjoying the stunning coastal scenery, this region is a must-visit for anyone exploring Western Australia.

The Kimberley Region: Gorges, Waterfalls, and Remote Wilderness

The Kimberley region, located in the northern part of Western Australia, is one of the last true wilderness areas on the planet. Renowned for its dramatic landscapes, including ancient gorges, stunning waterfalls, and vast savannahs, the Kimberley is a haven for adventure seekers and nature lovers. Spanning over 420,000 square kilometers, this rugged region is sparsely populated, allowing for an unspoiled wilderness experience that feels truly remote and wild.

One of the highlights of the Kimberley is **Bungle Bungles** (Purnululu National Park), a UNESCO World Heritage site known for its distinctive striped sandstone domes. The park offers a range of walking trails that lead to breathtaking viewpoints and ancient rock art sites. The

Piccaninny Gorge Walk is a popular choice, providing an opportunity to explore the stunning landscapes and spot unique wildlife along the way. Helicopter tours are also available, offering a bird's-eye view of the Bungle Bungles and the surrounding landscape, showcasing the vastness and beauty of this remote region.

The Kimberley is home to some of Australia's most spectacular waterfalls, particularly during the wet season from December to March. **Horizontal Falls**, located in **Talbot Bay**, is a natural phenomenon where tides rush through narrow gorges, creating a horizontal waterfall effect. Scenic flights and boat tours offer thrilling experiences to witness this incredible sight. **King George Falls**, one of the highest waterfalls in Australia, plunges 122 meters into a deep gorge, providing stunning views and a refreshing swimming spot during the dry season.

Exploring the **Gibb River Road** is another popular adventure in the Kimberley, offering access to some of the region's most remote landscapes. This iconic

660-kilometer track takes travelers through rugged terrain, allowing for exploration of gorges, cattle stations, and ancient rock art sites. Stops along the way include the picturesque **Bell Gorge**, known for its crystal-clear water and natural swimming holes, and the **Manning Gorge**, where visitors can swim beneath a stunning waterfall.

The rich Indigenous culture of the Kimberley adds depth to the region's natural beauty. The **Wandjina** and **Gwion Gwion** rock art, found in various locations throughout the region, provide a glimpse into the spiritual beliefs and history of the Indigenous people who have inhabited the area for thousands of years. Guided tours led by local Indigenous guides offer insights into their connection to the land, traditional practices, and stories that have been passed down through generations.

Due to its remote nature, accommodations in the Kimberley range from luxury lodges and eco-resorts to camping and caravan parks. **El Questro Wilderness Park** offers a unique experience with a variety of accommodations, from camping under the stars to luxurious homesteads. Visitors can explore the park's stunning landscapes, relax in thermal springs, and embark on guided tours to discover the region's natural wonders.

The Kimberley region is a place of breathtaking beauty and adventure, where visitors can immerse themselves in the rugged landscapes, experience the thrill of outdoor activities, and connect with the rich cultural heritage of Indigenous Australia. With its dramatic gorges, stunning waterfalls, and remote wilderness, the Kimberley is a destination that leaves a lasting impression on those who venture into its wild heart.

Ningaloo Reef: Swimming with Whale Sharks and Coral Coast Adventures

Ningaloo Reef, located on the Coral Coast of Western Australia, is one of the world's largest fringing reefs and a UNESCO World Heritage site. Renowned for its extraordinary marine biodiversity and vibrant coral gardens, Ningaloo offers unparalleled opportunities for snorkeling, diving, and swimming with some of the ocean's most magnificent creatures. The reef is easily accessible from the shore, making it a popular destination for both novice and experienced snorkelers and divers.

One of the main attractions of Ningaloo Reef is the chance to swim with **whale sharks**, the gentle giants of the ocean. These magnificent creatures, which can grow up to 18 meters long, migrate to the reef between March and July each year to feed on plankton. Numerous tour operators offer guided experiences that allow visitors to snorkel alongside these incredible animals, creating unforgettable memories in the crystal-clear waters of the reef. In addition to whale sharks, Ningaloo is home to a diverse array of marine life, including manta rays, turtles, and a vibrant variety of fish species, making it a paradise for underwater enthusiasts.

The stunning coastal scenery of Ningaloo is complemented by a range of outdoor activities beyond snorkeling and diving. **Cape Range National Park**, located adjacent to the reef, features breathtaking landscapes, rugged gorges, and pristine beaches. The **Yardie Creek** Gorge is a highlight of the park, offering opportunities for kayaking, hiking, and wildlife spotting. The diverse ecosystems within the park provide habitats for various species, including rock wallabies, emus, and numerous bird species.

For those seeking relaxation, the tranquil beaches along the Ningaloo Coast offer the perfect setting to unwind. **Coral Bay** is a charming coastal town known for its calm waters and stunning coral gardens, ideal for swimming and snorkeling right off the beach. **Exmouth**, another popular town in the region, serves as a gateway to Ningaloo Reef and offers a range of accommodations, dining options, and shops. Both towns provide a laid-back atmosphere and opportunities to connect with the local community.

The region is also rich in Indigenous culture, with local Aboriginal communities having a deep connection to the land and sea. Guided tours led by Indigenous guides provide insights into traditional practices, stories, and the significance of the natural environment. Engaging with these communities allows visitors to gain a deeper understanding of the cultural heritage of the region.

As night falls, the Ningaloo Coast transforms into a stargazer's paradise, with minimal light pollution providing stunning views of the night sky. Camping under the stars or enjoying a beachside bonfire allows visitors to connect with the natural beauty of the area and appreciate the tranquility of this remote location.

Chapter 7

EMERGENCY CONTACTS AND SAFETY INFORMATION

When traveling to Australia, being informed about emergency contacts and safety protocols is essential for ensuring a smooth and secure journey. Familiarizing yourself with local emergency numbers, such as **000** for police, ambulance, and fire services, can be a lifesaver in critical situations. It's also important to know the locations and contact details of your country's embassy or consulate in Australia, as they can provide crucial support in case of emergencies, such as lost passports, legal issues, or health crises. Additionally, understanding the healthcare system, including hospitals, clinics, and pharmacies, will allow you to seek prompt medical assistance if necessary. By preparing yourself with this information before your trip, you'll have the confidence to handle any unexpected situations that may arise.

Equally important is the role of travel insurance in safeguarding your trip. A comprehensive travel insurance policy can cover a wide range of potential issues, including medical emergencies, trip cancellations, lost luggage, and personal liability. Being aware of your coverage can prevent significant financial burdens in case of unforeseen events. It's advisable to read through your policy carefully to ensure it meets your travel needs, especially if you plan on engaging in adventure activities that may require additional coverage. Armed with knowledge of emergency contacts, health services, and the benefits of travel insurance, you'll be well-prepared to enjoy all that Australia has to offer while minimizing the impact of any unforeseen circumstances.

Emergency Numbers: Police, Ambulance, and Fire Services

Australia has a straightforward system for emergency contacts, with the national emergency number being **000**. This number can be dialed from any phone, including mobile devices, and connects you to emergency services, including police, ambulance, and fire services. It is vital to use this number only in genuine emergencies, as misuse can lead to penalties.

Police Services

In the event of a crime, accident, or any situation requiring police assistance, dialing **000** will dispatch local law enforcement to your location. You can also contact local police stations directly if you need to report a non-emergency incident. For more serious issues, such as theft, assault, or harassment, the police can provide immediate support. In major cities, you will find police stations in strategic locations, and many have a community outreach focus to assist tourists.

Ambulance Services

For medical emergencies, calling **000** will also summon an ambulance. Australia has a well-resourced ambulance service, and paramedics are highly trained to provide emergency medical care and transport patients to hospitals. Depending on the state, there may be associated fees for ambulance services, so it is important to check your health insurance policy to understand coverage in case of an emergency.

Fire Services

If you encounter a fire or need to report suspicious activities, dial **000** for the fire department. Fire services in Australia are equipped to handle a range of incidents, including bushfires, which can be common in certain areas during the summer months. Fire safety regulations are strictly enforced, so it's advisable to familiarize yourself with local fire safety measures and heed any warnings or advisories issued by local authorities.

Embassy and Consulate Contacts for International Travelers

For international travelers, knowing how to contact your country's embassy or consulate in Australia is essential, especially in case of emergencies such as lost passports, legal issues, or other unforeseen circumstances. Each country maintains diplomatic missions in major Australian cities.

Finding Your Embassy or Consulate

Most embassies are located in Canberra, Australia's capital city, but many countries also have consulates in Sydney, Melbourne, Brisbane, and Perth. It is advisable to keep the contact details of your embassy or consulate handy, including phone numbers, addresses, and emergency contact services. A comprehensive list of embassies and consulates is available on the website of the Department of Foreign Affairs and Trade of Australia, providing essential information for travelers.

Services Offered

Embassies and consulates can assist with various services, including issuing emergency travel documents, providing legal assistance, and helping with any crises involving their citizens. In the case of lost or stolen passports, embassy staff can guide you through the process of obtaining a replacement, which may involve reporting the theft to local police and completing necessary paperwork. Consulates can also assist in situations of illness or injury, providing a connection to local medical facilities and services.

Health Services: Hospitals, Clinics, and Pharmacies

Australia has a robust healthcare system, offering high-quality medical services across the country. Understanding how to access health services can be vital during your travels.

Hospitals

Public hospitals in Australia provide comprehensive emergency and inpatient care, and they are equipped to handle a wide range of medical emergencies. Major cities like Sydney, Melbourne, and Brisbane have several public hospitals offering 24-hour emergency services. If you need to go to a hospital, dial **000** for an ambulance or seek assistance to reach the nearest emergency department.

For less critical health issues, there are also private hospitals and clinics throughout the country. While public healthcare services are funded by the government, private hospitals may charge fees, so it's important to have appropriate health insurance coverage.

Medical Clinics

In addition to hospitals, Australia has numerous medical clinics that provide general health services, minor emergency care, and preventative health check-ups. Many clinics offer walk-in services, and some operate extended hours to accommodate travelers. It's advisable to call ahead to ensure the clinic can address your specific needs.

Pharmacies

Pharmacies are widely available in Australia, and they can be an excellent resource for travelers. Pharmacies can provide over-the-counter medications, health advice, and minor medical treatments. In case of a non-life-threatening health issue, visiting a pharmacy may be a convenient first step. Many pharmacists in Australia are trained to provide health advice and can recommend appropriate treatments for common ailments.

For prescription medications, be sure to bring a copy of your prescription, as well as a sufficient supply of any necessary medications to last for the duration of your trip. If you need a prescription filled while in Australia, pharmacies can help you, but it may require a consultation with a local healthcare provider.

Travel Insurance and What to Do in Case of Emergency

Travel insurance is an essential aspect of planning any trip, providing vital coverage for unexpected events that may occur while traveling. From medical emergencies and trip cancellations to lost luggage, having travel insurance can significantly alleviate the financial burden of unforeseen incidents.

Importance of Travel Insurance

Travel insurance varies in coverage and cost, so it's important to read the policy carefully and choose one that meets your specific needs. Look for policies that cover medical emergencies, trip interruptions, lost or stolen belongings, and personal liability. Ensure that the policy includes coverage for any activities you plan to undertake, especially if they involve higher risks, such as scuba diving or extreme sports.

What to Do in Case of Emergency

In the event of a medical emergency, first, seek appropriate help by calling **000** for ambulance services. If you are in a situation requiring the involvement of your embassy or consulate, reach out to them after ensuring your immediate safety. Keep a record of all communications, medical treatment received, and any expenses incurred during the emergency, as this information will be essential when filing a claim with your insurance provider.

In case of lost belongings or travel disruptions, report the issue to local authorities (for theft) and contact your travel insurance provider as soon as possible. They can guide you through the claims process and advise on the necessary steps to take.

Final Thoughts on Safety

Being prepared and informed is the key to ensuring a safe and enjoyable trip to Australia. Understanding the local emergency numbers, knowing how to contact your embassy or consulate, having access to healthcare services, and securing travel insurance can help mitigate risks and provide peace of mind during your travels. Familiarize yourself with this information before your trip and keep it readily available for easy access throughout your journey. By prioritizing your safety and well-being, you can focus on enjoying all that Australia has to offer, from its stunning landscapes to its vibrant culture.

Traveling to Western Australia offers remarkable experiences and breathtaking landscapes, but being prepared for emergencies is just as important as enjoying the journey itself. By understanding emergency contacts, health services, and the importance of travel insurance, you can navigate any unexpected situations with confidence. Keep this information handy, and ensure you have a plan in place for emergencies, allowing you to fully immerse yourself in the adventure of discovering Western Australia.

Chapter 8

BEST TIME TO VISIT AUSTRALIA

Australia's vastness and diversity create a unique tapestry of experiences that shift dramatically with the changing seasons. From the sun-soaked beaches of the Gold Coast and the rugged outback of the Northern Territory to the lush rainforests of Queensland and the vibrant cultural hubs of Sydney and Melbourne, each region offers something special at different times of the year. For instance, summer brings warm weather perfect for beach outings and outdoor festivals, while autumn introduces cooler temperatures that enhance the scenic beauty of places like the Blue Mountains and the wine regions. Winter offers opportunities for skiing in the Snowy Mountains and exploring the tropical north without the humidity, and spring breathes life into Australia's flora, making it an ideal time for wildflower enthusiasts and nature lovers. By understanding the seasonal patterns and climate variations across Australia, travelers can plan their trips to coincide with their desired activities and experiences, ensuring an enriching journey through this magnificent country.

In addition to the changing seasons, Australia boasts an array of unique wildlife experiences and cultural events that are best enjoyed during specific times of the year. Whale watching, for instance, peaks from May to November along the eastern coast, offering travelers a chance to witness these majestic creatures in their natural habitat. Similarly, turtle nesting occurs from November to March, primarily on the Great Barrier Reef's islands, allowing visitors to witness the miracle of life as hatchlings make their way to the ocean. Coupled with vibrant festivals like Sydney Festival in January and the Melbourne International Comedy Festival in March, travelers have the opportunity to immerse themselves in Australia's rich cultural fabric. By carefully selecting when to visit based on wildlife patterns, cultural events, and personal interests, travelers can create a tailored experience that showcases the very best of Australia throughout the year.

Australia's Seasons: A Breakdown of Climate and Regions

Australia experiences four distinct seasons: summer, autumn, winter, and spring. However, the timing and characteristics of these seasons vary significantly across the country due to its vast geographical size. Understanding the seasonal variations is key to planning your trip.

Summer (December to February)

In Australia, summer runs from December to February, with temperatures soaring in many regions, particularly in the northern parts. Coastal areas such as Sydney and Melbourne experience warm to hot weather, making this a peak time for beach activities, festivals, and outdoor events. However, it is essential to note that while southern cities are enjoying summer, northern regions like Darwin and Cairns will face the wet season, characterized by high humidity, heavy rains, and tropical storms. This time of year is perfect for enjoying water sports, barbecues, and vibrant city life, but travelers should prepare for the possibility of rain in the north.

Autumn (March to May)

Autumn, from March to May, is one of the most pleasant times to visit Australia, particularly in southern regions. With milder temperatures and less humidity, cities like Melbourne and Adelaide come alive with festivals and culinary events. This season also brings beautiful autumn foliage, especially in regions such as the Blue Mountains and the Yarra Valley. In the north, the weather begins to clear up, making it a great time for outdoor adventures and exploring the Great Barrier Reef.

Winter (June to August)

Winter in Australia occurs from June to August, bringing cooler temperatures, particularly in the southern states. Cities like Melbourne and Hobart can experience chilly weather, with temperatures dropping to single digits at night. This season is perfect for enjoying winter sports in regions such as the Snowy Mountains or Tasmania. Conversely, northern areas like Darwin and Cairns remain warm and dry, making it an ideal time to explore tropical regions and indulge in outdoor activities without the oppressive heat.

Spring (September to November)

Spring, spanning September to November, is marked by blossoming flowers and increasing temperatures across the country. This season is particularly beautiful in places like the Flinders Ranges and the Margaret River region, where wildflowers bloom, and vineyards come to life. Cities begin to warm up, making it an excellent time for outdoor festivals, food and wine events, and exploring natural attractions. Wildlife is also active during this time, offering opportunities for birdwatching and other nature-related activities.

When to Visit for Wildlife: Whale Watching, Turtle Nesting, and More

Australia is renowned for its diverse wildlife, and knowing the best times to witness these incredible animals in their natural habitats can significantly enhance your travel experience.

Whale Watching

The whale watching season in Australia generally runs from May to November, with the best opportunities for sightings occurring between July and September. During this time, humpback whales migrate along the eastern coast, providing thrilling viewing opportunities from locations such as Hervey Bay, Byron Bay, and Sydney. The southern right whales can also be observed along the southern coast, particularly in places like Warrnambool in Victoria. Special whale-watching tours are available, and knowledgeable guides can offer insights into the behaviors and habits of these magnificent creatures.

Turtle Nesting

Another remarkable wildlife experience is turtle nesting, which typically occurs from November to March. The Great Barrier Reef is a prime location for this phenomenon, particularly on the northern beaches and islands, such as Lady Elliot Island and Heron Island. Green turtles and loggerhead turtles come ashore to lay their eggs, and if you visit during the right time, you may witness hatchlings making their way to the sea. It is crucial to respect wildlife regulations and guidelines to protect these vulnerable species during this delicate process.

Bird Watching

For bird enthusiasts, spring is an excellent time to visit Australia, as many migratory bird species return to the country during this season. Wetlands and national parks, such as Kakadu National Park in the Northern Territory and the Adelaide International Bird Sanctuary, become hotspots for birdwatching. Additionally, many local communities celebrate birdwatching festivals that provide guided tours and opportunities to spot rare species.

Other Wildlife Encounters

Australia offers numerous other wildlife experiences year-round. For example, kangaroos and koalas can be spotted in their natural habitats in various national parks, including Kangaroo Island and the Grampians. For those interested in unique wildlife encounters, visiting during the spring and summer months increases the chances of seeing baby animals, such as joeys and ducklings, as many species breed during this time.

Events and Festivals: Timing Your Trip for Australia's Best Celebrations

Australia is home to a vibrant calendar of events and festivals, reflecting the country's diverse culture and heritage. Timing your visit to coincide with these celebrations can provide unforgettable experiences.

Sydney Festival (January)

Held every January, the Sydney Festival is a month-long celebration of art and culture that transforms the city into a vibrant stage. Featuring performances, exhibitions, and installations, the festival showcases local and international artists across various disciplines, including theater, dance, music, and visual arts. With free events and family-friendly activities, this festival attracts visitors from around the globe and offers a unique insight into Australia's cultural scene.

Vivid Sydney (May to June)

Vivid Sydney is a spectacular festival of light, music, and ideas that takes place from late May to early June. The city's iconic landmarks, such as the Sydney Opera House and Harbour Bridge, are illuminated with stunning light installations, creating a magical atmosphere. The festival also features a diverse program of music performances, talks, and workshops, making it an exciting time to visit the city.

Melbourne International Comedy Festival (March to April)

For those with a penchant for humor, the Melbourne International Comedy Festival, held from March to April, is one of the largest and most prestigious comedy festivals in the world. Featuring a lineup of local and international comedians, the festival includes stand-up performances, theater shows, and workshops. Visitors can enjoy a lively atmosphere filled with laughter while experiencing Melbourne's vibrant arts scene.

Queen's Birthday Weekend (June)

In June, Australia celebrates the Queen's Birthday, a public holiday marked by festivities and events across the country. Various regions host local festivals, markets, and cultural events during this long weekend, providing an excellent opportunity to immerse yourself in the community spirit. It is also a popular time for outdoor activities and gatherings, making it a great time to connect with locals.

Christmas and New Year Celebrations (December)

Australia's summer season culminates in festive celebrations for Christmas and New Year. Cities and towns are adorned with lights and decorations, and various events are held, including Christmas markets, concerts, and parades. Sydney's iconic New Year's Eve fireworks display over the Harbour is a world-renowned celebration that attracts thousands of visitors each year. It's a unique experience to celebrate the holidays in Australia's warm weather, enjoying beach barbecues and outdoor festivities.

Choosing the Perfect Time Based on Your Travel Style and Interests

Ultimately, the best time to visit Australia depends on your personal travel style, interests, and desired experiences. Whether you prefer outdoor adventures, cultural experiences, or wildlife encounters, planning your trip according to the season can enhance your enjoyment and satisfaction.

Adventure Seekers

For adventure enthusiasts, the cooler months of autumn and spring are ideal for exploring the great outdoors. This time offers comfortable temperatures for hiking in national parks, surfing along the coast, or embarking on road trips through Australia's stunning landscapes. Regions such as Tasmania and the Great Ocean Road are especially beautiful during these seasons, with fewer crowds and vibrant natural scenery.

Beach Lovers

If you're a beach lover, summer is the prime time to enjoy Australia's world-famous beaches. Coastal cities like Sydney, Brisbane, and Perth are bustling with activity, and the warm weather allows for a range of beach-related activities, from swimming and sunbathing to beach volleyball and surfing. However, be prepared for larger crowds and higher accommodation prices during peak holiday periods.

Culture Enthusiasts

For those seeking cultural experiences, aligning your visit with Australia's diverse festivals and events can enhance your trip. Each city offers a variety of cultural celebrations throughout the year, showcasing the arts, music, food, and heritage. Researching local events in advance and planning your itinerary around them will ensure you experience the best of Australia's cultural offerings.

Wildlife Observers

If witnessing Australia's unique wildlife is a priority, consider traveling during the specific seasons for activities such as whale watching, turtle nesting, or birdwatching. By timing your visit accordingly, you'll have the opportunity to observe these incredible natural events and engage with Australia's rich biodiversity.

Family Travelers

For families traveling with children, school holidays can impact travel plans. Consider planning your trip during the school holiday periods, which occur in December,

January, April, and September. However, be aware that popular tourist destinations may be busier and more expensive during these times. Look for family-friendly festivals and activities that provide engaging experiences for children, ensuring that everyone has a memorable trip.

Chapter 9

AUSTRALIA'S UNIQUE WILDLIFE AND NATURE

Australia's wildlife is truly one-of-a-kind, offering an extraordinary variety of species that have evolved in isolation over millions of years. From the arid Outback to the vibrant rainforests and pristine coastlines, Australia's diverse habitats are home to some of the world's most iconic creatures, including kangaroos, koalas, and wombats. These marsupials, which are synonymous with the country's identity, are just a glimpse into the remarkable biodiversity Australia has to offer. The country's ecosystems also support an impressive range of bird species, such as the colorful rainbow lorikeet and the powerful wedge-tailed eagle, as well as unique marine life like the dugong and the great white shark. Whether exploring the tropical rainforests of Queensland or the vast deserts of the Red Centre, visitors are bound to encounter wildlife that cannot be found anywhere else in the world, making Australia a must-visit destination for nature enthusiasts.

In addition to its iconic species, Australia is home to incredible conservation efforts that aim to preserve this rich biodiversity. Many of the country's native species, including the Tasmanian devil and the bilby, are under threat due to habitat destruction, invasive species, and climate change. In response, a range of organizations, from government bodies to grassroots initiatives, are working tirelessly to protect and restore critical habitats, as well as to rehabilitate endangered species. Conservation parks, wildlife sanctuaries, and national reserves are central to these efforts, allowing visitors to witness the beauty of Australia's wildlife while supporting its preservation. For travelers, the opportunity to experience Australia's flora and fauna is not only a thrilling adventure but also a chance to contribute to ongoing efforts to protect this natural heritage for future generations.

Meet the Marsupials: Kangaroos, Koalas, and Tasmanian Devils

Australia's most iconic wildlife includes its marsupials, a unique group of mammals known for their distinctive reproductive system, where young are born at a relatively undeveloped stage and continue to grow in the mother's pouch. Among these, kangaroos, koalas, and Tasmanian devils stand out as symbols of Australian fauna, each with their own fascinating traits and habitats.

Kangaroos

Kangaroos are perhaps the most recognized representatives of Australian wildlife. These agile herbivores are found in various habitats across the continent, from open grasslands and forests to arid regions. There are four main species: the red kangaroo, eastern gray kangaroo, western gray kangaroo, and antilopine kangaroo. Red kangaroos are the largest and can weigh up to 90 kilograms (200 pounds), capable of leaping over three meters (10 feet) in a single bound.

Kangaroos are social animals, often seen in groups called mobs, and they have a complex social structure. Their diet primarily consists of grasses and leaves, making them an integral part of Australia's ecosystem.

Koalas

Koalas are another beloved symbol of Australia, known for their adorable appearance and unique lifestyle. These tree-dwelling marsupials are primarily found in eucalyptus forests along the eastern and southeastern coasts of Australia. Koalas have a specialized diet, relying almost exclusively on eucalyptus leaves, which are toxic to most animals. To cope with their low-energy diet, koalas sleep for up to 18 hours a day, conserving energy for their foraging activities during the early morning and late afternoon. Their populations face significant threats from habitat loss, bushfires, and disease, leading to increased conservation efforts aimed at protecting their natural habitats and ensuring their survival.

Tasmanian Devils

The Tasmanian devil, a carnivorous marsupial native to Tasmania, is known for its stocky build and ferocious feeding habits. These nocturnal scavengers primarily consume carrion, using their powerful jaws and teeth to crack bones and eat the entire carcass. Unfortunately, the Tasmanian devil has faced severe population declines due to a transmissible cancer known as Devil Facial Tumor Disease (DFTD), which has decimated wild populations. Conservation programs are underway to breed Tasmanian devils in captivity and reintroduce them into disease-free areas, helping to ensure the survival of this unique species.

Birdwatching in Australia: From Parrots to Penguins

Australia's avian diversity is impressive, boasting over 800 species of birds, making it a paradise for birdwatchers. The continent's varied habitats provide opportunities to observe both endemic and migratory species, ranging from brightly colored parrots and cockatoos to unique seabirds and penguins.

Parrots and Cockatoos

Among Australia's most vibrant bird species are its parrots and cockatoos, which are known for their striking plumage and intelligence. The iconic rainbow lorikeet, with its bright green, blue, and orange feathers, is a common sight in urban areas and gardens. Similarly, the sulfur-crested cockatoo, recognizable by its distinctive yellow crest, can often be found in both urban and rural settings. These birds are highly social and can often be seen in large flocks, engaging in playful behaviors. Their intelligence and vocal abilities make them popular among bird enthusiasts and pet owners alike.

Seabirds and Penguins

Australia's coastlines are home to an array of seabirds, including gulls, pelicans, and albatrosses. One of the most endearing seabirds is the little penguin, the world's smallest species of penguin, which can be found along the southern coasts of Australia, particularly at Phillip Island. Each evening, visitors can witness the "penguin parade" as these adorable birds return to shore after a day of foraging in the ocean. Other notable seabirds include the Australian pelican, known for its large bill and impressive wingspan, and the wedge-tailed shearwater, which nests on islands along the coast.

Birdwatching Destinations

For avid birdwatchers, Australia offers a multitude of prime birdwatching locations. Kakadu National Park in the Northern Territory is renowned for its diverse birdlife, where visitors can spot species such as the jabiru, brolga, and whistling kite. The wetlands of the Top End are particularly rich in birdlife, especially during the migratory season. In the southeast, the coast of New South Wales features coastal wetlands and bushland, attracting a variety of birds, while the rainforests of Queensland are home to unique species such as the cassowary and lyrebird.

Aquatic Wonders: Dolphins, Dugongs, and Marine Life

Australia's marine environment is just as rich and diverse as its terrestrial ecosystems. With an extensive coastline and world-renowned coral reefs, the country offers countless opportunities to explore its vibrant underwater world. From playful dolphins to the gentle dugong and an array of colorful marine life, Australia's oceans are teeming with wonders.

Dolphins

Dolphins are among the most charismatic marine mammals found along Australia's coasts. Species such as the bottlenose dolphin and the common dolphin can be spotted in various locations, including bays, estuaries, and coastal waters. Popular dolphin-watching destinations include Port Stephens in New South Wales, where visitors can enjoy boat tours to observe these playful creatures in their natural habitat. In addition to boat tours, some locations, such as Monkey Mia in

Western Australia, offer opportunities for visitors to interact with dolphins as they come to shore for feeding.

Dugongs

Dugongs, often referred to as "sea cows," are herbivorous marine mammals that graze on seagrass beds in shallow coastal waters. These gentle creatures are primarily found in the warm waters of the Great Barrier Reef and along the northern coast of Australia. Dugongs are protected under Australian law, and conservation efforts are underway to safeguard their habitats and ensure their survival. Snorkeling and diving in areas like Hervey Bay and Moreton Bay provide a chance to observe these magnificent creatures up close as they feed on seagrass.

Coral Reefs and Marine Life

Australia is home to the Great Barrier Reef, the largest coral reef system in the world, which is renowned for its incredible biodiversity. This UNESCO World Heritage Site is home to thousands of marine species, including colorful corals, fish, sea turtles, and sharks. Snorkeling and diving are popular activities that allow visitors to explore the vibrant underwater world, with numerous tour operators offering excursions to the reef. Other marine parks, such as Ningaloo Reef in Western Australia, provide similar experiences, with opportunities to swim with whale sharks and spot manta rays.

Conservation of Marine Environments

Australia's marine environments face significant threats from climate change, pollution, and overfishing. Conservation organizations and government initiatives are working diligently to protect these vital ecosystems. Marine protected areas (MPAs) have been established along the coasts to safeguard biodiversity and ensure sustainable use of marine resources. Efforts to restore seagrass beds, promote responsible fishing practices, and mitigate the impacts of climate change are crucial for preserving Australia's aquatic wonders for future generations.

Conservation Efforts: Protecting Australia's Endangered Species

Australia's unique wildlife faces numerous threats, including habitat loss, climate change, invasive species, and diseases. Conservation efforts are essential for protecting the country's endangered species and preserving its biodiversity. Various organizations, government agencies, and community groups are actively engaged in initiatives to conserve and rehabilitate wildlife and their habitats.

Habitat Conservation

One of the primary focuses of conservation efforts in Australia is habitat protection and restoration. Deforestation, land clearing, and urban development have led to significant loss of natural habitats for many species. Protected areas, such as national parks and wildlife reserves, play a crucial role in safeguarding biodiversity. The Australian government has established a network of protected areas that encompass diverse ecosystems, ensuring that wildlife has safe havens to thrive. Community-led initiatives, such as tree-planting projects and habitat restoration programs, also contribute to rebuilding natural habitats and supporting local wildlife populations.

Species Recovery Programs

Various species recovery programs aim to address the specific needs of endangered species. These programs often involve captive breeding, habitat restoration, and monitoring of wild populations. For example, the recovery plan for the critically endangered Western Ground Parrot focuses on habitat restoration and predator control to increase the chances of survival for this rare bird. Similarly, efforts to conserve the Greater Bilby have included breeding programs, habitat restoration, and community engagement initiatives to raise awareness about the species' plight.

Community Involvement

Engaging local communities in conservation efforts is vital for fostering a sense of stewardship and connection to the environment. Education programs, citizen science initiatives, and volunteer opportunities empower individuals to contribute to conservation efforts. Organizations such as Landcare encourage communities to take an active role in protecting and restoring their local environments. By fostering a culture of conservation and environmental awareness, Australia can work towards a more sustainable future for its wildlife.

Indigenous Knowledge and Conservation

Australia's Indigenous peoples have a profound connection to the land and possess valuable traditional ecological knowledge that can enhance conservation efforts. Collaborating with Indigenous communities can lead to more effective management of natural resources and habitats. Programs that integrate traditional land management practices, such as controlled burning and sustainable hunting, have shown promise in enhancing biodiversity and promoting healthy ecosystems.

Chapter 10

DOS AND DON'TS IN AUSTRALIA

Traveling to Australia is an adventure that promises stunning landscapes, vibrant cities, and encounters with unique wildlife, but it also requires an understanding of the country's cultural and environmental dynamics. Australia is home to a relaxed and friendly culture, where locals value politeness, humility, and a "no worries" attitude in daily interactions. However, this laid-back approach doesn't mean that tourists can ignore important social customs and safety precautions. Respecting personal space, being punctual, and adhering to road rules are key expectations when navigating Australian society. The country's diverse climate, ranging from the tropical north to the cooler southern regions, also demands careful planning, particularly in terms of sun protection and hydration. This chapter will guide you through these cultural nuances, offering tips on how to engage with locals, safely explore the country's vast terrain, and make the most of your experience without offending or inconveniencing others.

In addition to cultural etiquette, understanding Australia's environmental sensitivities and Indigenous heritage is crucial for any responsible traveler. The country's vast wilderness, from the iconic Outback to the Great Barrier Reef, is beautiful but fragile, requiring visitors to follow guidelines that protect these ecosystems. Whether it's respecting wildlife, avoiding environmental damage at the beaches, or being mindful of sacred Indigenous sites like Uluru, tourists must approach their journey with a sense of responsibility and respect for the land. Many common tourist mistakes—such as underestimating the dangers posed by wildlife, ignoring quarantine regulations, or failing to conserve water—can easily be avoided with proper preparation. This chapter will highlight not only what to avoid but also how to contribute positively to Australia's environment and local communities through sustainable practices, making your visit as enriching for the destination as it is for you.

Dos for an Enjoyable Australian Trip: Cultural Etiquette and Safety Tips

1. Be Friendly and Casual in Conversations

Australians are known for their laid-back, friendly demeanor, and they appreciate this in return. Engage in polite small talk and don't hesitate to greet people with a smile. While Australians are easygoing, they also value humility. Bragging or boastful behavior is generally frowned upon, so it's better to be down-to-earth in your interactions.

2. Respect Personal Space

Personal space is important in Australia. Whether you're standing in a queue or chatting with someone, keep a comfortable distance, as physical closeness can make people uncomfortable. Australians generally avoid physical contact like hugging or kissing unless they know someone well.

3. Embrace the "No Worries" Attitude

The quintessential Australian phrase "no worries" sums up a lot of the country's relaxed culture. If you encounter minor issues or delays, it's best to adopt this attitude. Stressing over small problems won't go over well, as Australians generally prefer to keep things light and unhurried.

4. Know the Road Rules

Australia is a vast country with many travelers opting for road trips. If you plan to drive, it's crucial to follow the road rules strictly. Australians drive on the left side of the road, and strict enforcement of traffic laws, including speed limits and driving under the influence, is common. Make sure to always wear a seatbelt and familiarize yourself with local driving laws.

5. Be Prepared for the Weather

Australia is known for its diverse climate. From the scorching heat of the Outback to the cooler temperatures in the south, it's essential to pack accordingly and stay sun-smart. Sunscreen, hats, and sunglasses are essential, as Australia's sun can be incredibly harsh. Hydrate often, especially if you're spending time outdoors, to avoid dehydration.

6. Use Appropriate Beach Etiquette

Australia's beaches are world-famous, but they also come with their own set of rules. Always swim between the red and yellow flags, which indicate areas monitored by lifeguards. Respect the ocean and pay attention to signs warning about dangerous currents or marine life. Public beaches are often alcohol-free zones, so check local laws before bringing any drinks to the sand.

7. Tipping is Optional but Appreciated

Unlike some countries where tipping is expected, in Australia it's generally not obligatory. However, tipping is appreciated, especially in restaurants, bars, or cafes when service is exceptional. Leaving around 10% is common, but if tipping isn't done, it's not considered rude or inappropriate.

8. Respect Environmental Regulations

Australia is highly protective of its environment, and many places have strict regulations to preserve natural beauty. Don't litter, and follow rules around wildlife interaction, such as not feeding animals in national parks. Many areas have designated paths to prevent damaging flora, and it's important to stick to these paths.

9. Understand the Public Transport System

In major cities like Sydney and Melbourne, the public transport system is reliable and affordable. Buses, trains, and ferries are well-maintained and user-friendly, but in rural areas, transport options may be limited. Buy a transport card, such as the Opal card in Sydney, and always tap on and off when boarding.

10. Be Aware of the "Outback" Challenges

If you're heading into the Outback, prepare meticulously. The distances between towns are vast, and mobile phone coverage can be limited. Always carry plenty of water, fuel, and a detailed map. Let someone know your travel itinerary, as getting stranded without help can be life-threatening.

Don'ts: Common Tourist Mistakes and How to Avoid Them

1. Don't Underestimate the Wildlife

Australia's wildlife is unique, but it can also be dangerous. From venomous snakes and spiders to crocodiles in the northern regions, it's important not to approach or disturb wild animals. In the ocean, be aware of jellyfish, sharks, and stingrays. If swimming in Northern Australia, check whether there are stinger nets during jellyfish season, and follow local advice on water safety.

2. Don't Ignore Indigenous Protocols

Australia is home to one of the world's oldest living cultures, and respecting Indigenous communities and customs is vital. Some places, like Uluru, are sacred to Indigenous Australians, and while tourism is welcomed in many areas, there are rules around behavior, such as not climbing certain landmarks or trespassing on sacred sites. Always ask for permission and follow guidelines if visiting Indigenous lands.

3. Don't Be Late

Punctuality is expected in professional settings and even in social engagements. If you're meeting someone or have a booking, aim to be on time or a little early. Australians are generally not too formal, but lateness without notice can be seen as disrespectful.

4. Don't Forget to Quarantine Items

Australia has strict biosecurity laws to protect its unique environment from pests and diseases. If you're entering the country, declare any food, plant material, or animal products. Bringing in prohibited items without declaring them can lead to heavy fines.

5. Don't Disregard the Water Conservation Efforts

Water is a precious resource in Australia, particularly in drier regions. Be mindful of your water use, especially during drought conditions. Shorter showers, avoiding wasting tap water, and reporting any leaks or problems in accommodation are all part of being a responsible traveler.

6. Don't Take Offense to Directness

Australians are typically straightforward and won't shy away from sharing their opinions. This directness isn't meant to be rude, but rather part of their candid communication style. Take it in stride and avoid taking it personally if someone is blunt with you.

7. Don't Smoke in Public Places

Smoking laws are strict in Australia. Smoking is banned in all indoor public areas, including restaurants, bars, and clubs. There are also restrictions on smoking in outdoor dining areas, public transport stops, and near playgrounds. Always check for designated smoking zones before lighting up.

8. Don't Expect Free Wi-Fi Everywhere

While many cafes, hotels, and restaurants offer free Wi-Fi, it's not as universally available in Australia as it is in other countries. Public Wi-Fi is more common in major cities but can be slow or limited in more remote areas. Consider purchasing a local SIM card for more reliable mobile data access.

9. Don't Skip Travel Insurance

Australia is a safe country, but accidents can happen, and healthcare for non-residents can be expensive. Comprehensive travel insurance is essential to cover potential medical emergencies, accidents, or lost belongings.

10. Don't Walk on the Reef

Australia's Great Barrier Reef is a fragile ecosystem. Walking on the coral, standing on it, or touching it can cause lasting damage. When snorkeling or diving, be cautious about where you place your feet and avoid disturbing marine life.

Respecting Indigenous Culture and Nature: What Every Visitor Should Know

1. Engage with Indigenous Experiences

Australia offers many opportunities to learn about Indigenous culture. From art galleries showcasing Aboriginal artwork to cultural tours led by Indigenous guides, taking part in these activities is an enriching way to appreciate the history and traditions of the land's First Peoples. Always approach these experiences with respect and a willingness to listen.

2. Understand the Significance of Sacred Sites

Many of Australia's most famous natural landmarks, such as Uluru and Kata Tjuta, hold deep spiritual significance for the Indigenous communities. Always follow the guidelines set by these communities, which might include not climbing or photographing certain sites. When in doubt, ask for permission or guidance.

3. Learn About Local Languages and Traditions

Australia's Indigenous culture is not monolithic, and different regions have their own languages and customs. Learning a few words or understanding the significance of specific practices can deepen your understanding and respect during your visit. Many areas have cultural centers where you can learn more about local traditions and history.

4. Support Indigenous-Owned Businesses

When buying souvenirs or local goods, consider supporting Indigenous-owned businesses. Look for art, crafts, and products that are authentically Indigenous-made and help sustain communities. This not only ensures you're taking home a piece of genuine culture but also supports economic sustainability in Indigenous regions.

5. Respect Local Wildlife

Australia's native animals, such as kangaroos, koalas, and dingoes, play a crucial role in the country's ecosystems. Observe wildlife from a distance and never attempt to touch or feed animals in the wild. Feeding wildlife can cause them to become dependent on human food, which is harmful to their health and survival.

6. Follow Leave-No-Trace Principles

When visiting natural areas, especially in national parks or on remote trails, it's essential to follow Leave-No-Trace principles. This means taking all of your waste with you, staying on marked trails to avoid damaging the environment, and avoiding disturbing the wildlife. Keep the natural beauty of Australia intact for future generations.

7. Be Conscious of Land Ownership

In many parts of Australia, the land is co-managed with Indigenous custodians. It's important to be mindful that you may be on private or traditionally-owned land, even when in remote areas. Follow all posted signs and instructions regarding land use, access, and behavior.

Practical Tips for Sustainable and Responsible Travel in Australia

1. Use Eco-Friendly Accommodation

Australia is home to a growing number of eco-friendly accommodations, ranging from luxury eco-lodges to sustainable camping sites. These properties focus on reducing their environmental impact through energy efficiency, water conservation, and waste management practices. Choose places that align with these principles to support green tourism.

2. Minimize Your Carbon Footprint

Australia's large size means air travel is often necessary, but consider alternative forms of transport where possible. Public transport, cycling, or even walking are eco-friendlier options for exploring cities and regional areas. When flying, consider offsetting your carbon emissions through verified programs.

3. Be Water-Wise

As mentioned, water is a scarce resource in many parts of Australia, particularly in arid regions. Take short showers, reuse towels in hotels, and avoid unnecessary water consumption to help conserve this vital resource. Some regions may have water restrictions in place, so be aware and follow local guidelines.

4. Reduce Plastic Waste

Plastic waste is a major environmental concern globally, and Australia is no exception. Carry a reusable water bottle, shopping bag, and utensils to minimize single-use plastic consumption during your travels. Many cafes and restaurants offer incentives for customers using their own cups or containers.

5. Respect Marine Life and Coral Reefs

If you're visiting coastal areas, especially the Great Barrier Reef, make sure you use reef-safe sunscreen to prevent harmful chemicals from damaging marine ecosystems. When diving or snorkeling, avoid touching the coral, and ensure you leave the underwater environment as pristine as you found it.

6. Participate in Conservation Programs

Many tour operators and national parks offer opportunities for visitors to get involved in conservation efforts. Whether it's helping to plant native trees, joining a beach clean-up, or supporting wildlife rehabilitation centers, these activities offer a hands-on way to give back to the environment while traveling.

7. Support Local Communities

When purchasing goods, dining out, or booking tours, choose local businesses over international chains. This not only supports the local economy but also fosters a deeper connection to the places you're visiting. Seek out locally-made products and services that reflect the region's character.

8. Educate Yourself on Australia's Environmental Challenges

Before traveling, take time to learn about the environmental challenges Australia faces, such as drought, bushfires, and the impact of climate change on its ecosystems. Understanding these issues will help you travel more mindfully and make choices that have a positive impact on the places you visit.

9. Offset Your Environmental Impact

Many companies and airlines now offer carbon offset options to neutralize the environmental footprint of your travel. Investing in these programs, particularly those verified by credible organizations, can help mitigate the environmental cost of your trip.

10. Be a Responsible Traveler Year-Round

Responsible travel isn't limited to when you're on holiday. Consider incorporating eco-conscious habits into your everyday life, such as reducing energy consumption, supporting conservation initiatives, and advocating for sustainable tourism policies in your home country.

Traveling to Australia offers an incredible opportunity to experience diverse landscapes, vibrant cities, and rich cultural heritage. By following the dos and avoiding the don'ts, and by being respectful of the Indigenous communities and the environment, you'll not only have a more enriching travel experience but also contribute to preserving the beauty and vitality of this unique country for generations to come.

Printed in Great Britain
by Amazon